STRATFORD
ITS HERITAGE AND ITS FESTIVAL

Carolynn Bart-Riedstra and Lutzen H. Riedstra
Contemporary photography by Terry Manzo
Foreword by Richard Monette

JAMES LORIMER & COMPANY LTD., PUBLISHERS
TORONTO 1999

James Lorimer & Company acknowledges the sup-port of the Department of Canadian Heritage and the Ontario Arts Council in the development of writing and publishing in Canada. We acknowledge the support of the Canada Council for the Arts for our publishing program.

This book is dedicated to our son, Lutzen Andries Richard Riedstra, whose patience was appreciated during the writing of our book and who even offered to stay home from daycare to help us.

Canadian Cataloguing in Publication Data

Bart-Riedstra, Carolynn, 1957-
Stratford: Its Heritage and Its Festival

Includes index.
ISBN 1-55028-634-X

1. Stratford (Ont.) - History. 2. Stratford (Ont.) - Tours. I. Riedstra, Lutzen H. II. Title.

FC3099.S77B37 1998 971.3'23 C98-932745-0
F1059.5.S78B37 1998

James Lorimer & Company Ltd., Publishers
35 Britain Street
Toronto, Ontario
M5A 1R7

Printed and bound in Canada

ACKNOWLEDGEMENTS

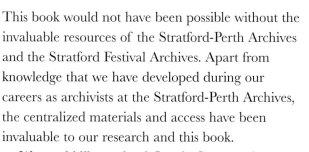

This book would not have been possible without the invaluable resources of the Stratford-Perth Archives and the Stratford Festival Archives. Apart from knowledge that we have developed during our careers as archivists at the Stratford-Perth Archives, the centralized materials and access have been invaluable to our research and this book.

We would like to thank Lynda Greve and especially Brandi Borman from the Stratford-Perth Archives for all of their help while we were writing this book. A special thank you to Lisa Brant and Jane Edmonds from the Stratford Festival Archives for their support and invaluable assistance with the festival chapter and to Ruth Mountford, photographer. We are indebted to Florence Patterson and Bruce Swerdfager for their time in talking with us about the festival. We'd also like to thank Robert Pearce of the London Museum of Archaeology for the loan of visual material and for his helpful comments, Karen VandenBrink of the Stratford-Perth Museum for access to items in the museum's collection, Wilf Gregory for the information he provided about the industrial period during the 1950s, Art Boon for generously permitting us to photograph his collection of articles from World Wars I and II, and David Prosser of the Stratford Festival for his comments on Chapter 5. Finally, we would like to thank our copy editor and proofreader, Jennifer Hutchison, and our editor, Diane Young, for her assistance, encouragement and patience.

This book would also not have been possible without the information collected by the historians of Stratford who have preceded us. Acknowledgement and thanks are given to R. Thomas Orr, Stafford Johnston, T. J. Dolan, Jim Anderson and Stan Dingman.

CONTENTS

Stratford Perth Archives

Funded by the City of Stratford and the County of Perth

MAR 0 6 2000

March 1, 2000

Hi Dorothy,

Sorry it has taken so long to get this book to you. We have had a very hectic January and February and I finally able to get back to doing the things I have not had time for.

I hope that you like this book. It is available at book stores and sells for $16.95 plus GST. If you would like to have it reviewed, that would be great but this copy is for you with our best wishes.

Take care.

Sincerely,

Carolyn

Carolynn Bart-Riedstra

233 Jormans Ave

N5A 6R5

FOREWORD

"What's in a name?" asks Juliet in William Shakespeare's *Romeo and Juliet*. And though she insists "that which we call a rose/By any other word would smell as sweet," the outcome of the play leaves little doubt that sometimes destiny can be embodied in a name. Had Romeo not been a Montague, a name hateful to the Capulets, he and Juliet might have lived to enjoy a happy old age. And had the directors of the Canada Company, in the first half of the nineteenth century, bestowed a different name on the settlement that became Stratford, Ontario, would this charming but unassuming little town, tucked away amid the farmlands of southwestern Ontario, have become the home of North America's largest classical repertory theatre?

But it was called Stratford from the start, and some form of spiritual connection with its namesake in Warwickshire, England—and with that other Stratford's most famous son—seems always to have been on the agenda. The river that runs through the community, once known as the Little Thames, was renamed the Avon as soon as the town's name was decided, and the first pub was to be called nothing less illustrious than The Shakespeare Inn. And when the growing settlement achieved the status of a town at the end of the 1850s, its five electoral wards were given Shakespearean names—Avon, Falstaff, Hamlet, Shakespeare and Romeo. The nearby village of Bell's Corners had already gotten into the act by changing its name to Shakespeare.

That sense of a special connection to the Bard of Avon and his birthplace was cherished even beyond

An aerial view of the Festival Theatre

the bounds of Stratford—beyond those, indeed, of Canada. As Carolynn Bart-Riedstra and Lutzen H. Riedstra recount in their absorbing portrait of this remarkable community, the third centenary of Shakespeare's birth was celebrated here on April 23, 1864. I happen to have in my possession a photocopy of a page from the *Boston Post* from April 6 of that year, in which the writer, having first posed the rhetorical question "Who publishes or reads a Canadian book?" and admitted, with an implicit shrug, that "we can hardly answer it with any confidence of correctness," commented enthusiastically, if a bit loftily, on Stratford's forthcoming festivities:

> The Canadians are, however, undoubtedly a reading people. They are a constituent part of the British Empire; although they may have no colonial literature, they may justly claim a part interest and part right in the literature of the mother country, and that is the most splendid body of letters ever bequeathed to man.

Shakespeare is, therefore, their countryman. They may rightly claim him and boast of him. They have not heretofore been unmindful of this, and are not now forgetful of the duties entailed and the trust imposed. They have the town of Stratford and the river Avon: hence their Stratford-upon-Avon. This town is to celebrate the approaching 300th anniversary of the poet's birth, by services worthy of the occasion. On the afternoon of the 23rd inst., at 2 o'clock, a splendid oak will be planted by the Mayor in the presence of the people, in the public plot, to be known hereafter as Shakespeare square. This ceremonial is to be followed by a regatta on the river Avon, and in the evening there is to be a jubilee oration, with Shakespearean recitations, and a Shakespeare ball. We hail this Canadian Stratford-upon-Avon as fully up to the spirit and the inspiration of the illustrious name it bears.

It is true that it took another ninety years, a crisis in the local economy and the determined vision of Stratford native Tom Patterson to realize the full potential of that inspiration, with the creation of the Stratford Shakespearean Festival Foundation of Canada. But even in 1952, the idea of a theatre festival in Stratford was not entirely new. Two decades earlier, in 1934, the local paper had carried a report of a dinner meeting of the local Rotary Club, at which J. Campbell McInnes, a visiting music adjudicator from Toronto, "suggested that Stratford should have a Summer Dramatic and Musical Festival, with the city's park system as a setting."

All of which might suggest that there is, in the lives of cities as well as of individuals, "a divinity that shapes our ends/Rough-hew them how we will." Sooner or later, Stratford and Shakespeare were bound to try and make a go of it together.

But, as Carolynn and Lutzen's book clearly demonstrates, there has always been far more to Stratford than an evocative name and an idyllic setting, and the advent of the festival has been only one milestone in the town's rich and colourful history. Those who know Stratford only for its theatre, its restaurants, its B&Bs and all the other amenities that sustain and are sustained by the $125-million-a-year visitor economy will enjoy this thoroughly fascinating account of a community that has had more than one claim to fame.

Many of the festival's visitors can name the celebrities who have graced our stages over the years: Alec Guinness, James Mason, Christopher Plummer, William Shatner, Maggie Smith and a host of others. But how many of them, I wonder, know that another well-known individual—not an actor or director but an inventor and entrepreneur— also lived for a time in Stratford? He began his career at age sixteen as a night telegraph operator at Stratford's railway station. He left under a cloud a few months later, after devising an automated signalling device that allowed him to sleep on the job. The young man's name was Thomas Alva Edison.

Carolynn and Lutzen remind us, too, that

The Shakespearean Gardens

Stratford made a memorable contribution to the world of professional hockey in the person of Howie Morenz, the "Stratford Streak." In his career with the Montreal Canadiens, Morenz became the most celebrated player of his generation, and his premature death in 1937, following a devastating injury on the rink, prompted a national outpouring of grief.

This book portrays a town that has always been determined to take charge of its own destiny. It was the coming of the railways in the 1850s that first put Stratford on the map and created its first major wave of wealth, and it was the decline of the locomotive industry in the early 1950s that motivated the city's concerned residents to look for a new economic base. That they should think of a theatre was not so strange, for there had always been people here with the interest, the will and the commitment to see the arts flourish. This was a town already accustomed to performances of plays, concerts, recitals and operettas, and the local newspaper's effusion about festival founder Tom Patterson's dream of Stratford as an "even greater" cultural centre may not have sounded as naively boosterish in the early 1950s—when there was very little professional theatre anywhere in the country—as it does today.

Fate may well have decreed a festival for Stratford, but that decree could not have been carried out without an incredible act of collective civic will. Tom Patterson's dream would have come to nothing had it not captured the imaginations of others in the community, such as Harrison Showalter, Alf and Dama Bell and all the others who spearheaded the drive to turn it into a reality. When a

fundraising campaign was launched to mount the first season in 1953, the citizens of Stratford dug deeply into their own pockets. In just four days, they contributed an amazing $42,000 toward the new festival. To put that in perspective, the most that had ever been raised in Stratford before was $18,000—and that was for the Red Cross in wartime. In the end, just under half of all the money raised for that first season came from Stratford's residents.

Oliver Gaffney, the contractor hired to build the concrete amphitheatre over which the initial canvas tent would be pitched, came to the rescue during the fledgling festival's darkest hour. When the money ran out and it seemed as if the whole project was going to collapse, Gaffney kept his crews working round the clock, not knowing when—or if—he'd be paid. Other local businesses showed themselves solidly behind the festival. Many pitched in to meet some of the novel requirements posed by the new theatre's prop-makers. Workers at James Preston's furniture factory, for instance, turned their hands to creating the huge fifteenth-century-style crucifixes used in the first season's production of *Richard III*.

This is not to say there weren't any tensions between the existing Stratford residents and the strange new playhouse creatures who suddenly arrived in their midst, or that those tensions did not persist for quite some time. I can remember in 1967, my third season at the festival, walking along the sidewalk and bumping into—or, more accurately, being bumped into by—a child of four or five years old. Certain that the responsibility for the collision was mine, the child glared at me and, red

Perth County Court House from the Avon River

with fury, shouted at me the worst name he could think of: "You . . . You . . . You *actor*!"

But over time, the theatre has become not only a major economic engine for the community but also a part of the fabric of its life. Many of its artists have bought houses here, and more than one generation of residents have worked at the festival or given their time as volunteers. The theatre has become a fact of Stratford life. And as a Stratford homeowner since 1977, I know that my fellow residents—and not just those who depend on the festival for a living—are proud of that fact.

For the Stratford Festival has been more than just a source of income. It has made a major contribution to the art of performing Shakespeare in our time. Its original thrust stage, proposed by Tyrone Guthrie and designed by Tanya Moiseiwitsch, revolutionized how we play Shakespeare, and its influence has been felt all through the Western world. That stage was designed to be used without scenery. Finding themselves having to rely on the spoken word, actors had to propel the verse with immense energy. Suddenly, productions of Shakespeare could move—indeed, *had* to move—with great speed and momentum: the same momentum, in fact, that underlies the text. Our thrust stage—since emulated in such other venues as the Chichester Festival Theatre, the Lincoln Centre, the Royal National Theatre and the Guthrie Theatre—allows performances today to be as powerful as they were in Shakespeare's time.

Stratford has also been the place where we have been able to give the classics a uniquely Canadian voice. We were able to do this, in part, because we had no past tradition to forbid it. There was, after all, a time not so long ago when a Stratford Festival production of a Shakespeare play might well be the first that had ever been mounted professionally in the history of this country. I remember Martha Henry saying to me, when we were acting together in the 1977 production of *All's Well That Ends Well*: "It's like discovering a new play." And indeed it was. Unencumbered by past production history, we were free to make those plays our own, to speak the verse in our own Canadian voices and to fulfill the promise of Cassius's words in *Julius Caesar*: "How many ages hence/Shall this our lofty scene be acted over/In states unborn and accents yet unknown!"

We can, of course, go too far in this direction. I remember a production of *Twelfth Night* in which Butch Blake played the Sea Captain. Instead of responding to Viola's question "What country, friends, is this?" with the line "This is Illyria, lady," I heard Butch say quite distinctly, "This is Orillia, lady."

And if Stratford has cause to be proud of its festival, so the festival has ample cause to be proud of its city. As you will find in the pages that follow, Stratford's story has itself been something of a drama, with its local heroes and villains, its sudden reversals of fortune, its good times and its bad—and through it all, an exemplary confidence in its own sense of identity. This is a city where art and life coexist as equal partners, where imagination and reality come together.

My predecessor as Artistic Director at the festival, David William, once said, "Stratford is one of the things that Canada has done right." He was talking about the theatre, but his words can just as easily bear the wider meaning. Certainly I, who have spent more of my life in Stratford than anywhere else, have no doubt at all that this auspiciously named city has succeeded in getting things gloriously, wonderfully right—and I shall always be proud to call it my home.

Richard Monette

INTRODUCTION

Stratford is situated in the centre of southwestern Ontario on the Avon River in the County of Perth. In the nineteenth century the town prospered as the hub for two railways—the Grand Trunk and the Buffalo and Lake Huron lines. In the first half of the twentieth century it had a booming furniture industry. Today it is best known for its world-famous Shakespearean Festival, which draws over half a million people to the city annually.

The Avon River

ialized commercialism and maintained its connections with its identity in the past as it moves into the future.

Visitors to Stratford today are attracted by the charm of the city. Its well-kept parks, Victorian houses and buildings and many restaurants and shops create the perfect setting for its famous theatre and combine to make Stratford one of the major tourist destinations in Canada from May until November each year.

But Stratford has another side as well which plays

As it has grown, Stratford has developed an ever closer connection with the identity it was given in its original name—Stratford-on-Avon. It has nurtured its association with Shakespeare without resorting to triv-

just as important a role in the city's well-being. Dominated by railway shops and furniture factories until the 1950s, Stratford has since become diversified with a strong automotive presence. Most of the city's workforce are employed in these industries. Visitors may see the city as an "arts" haven, but it is much more diverse than this. There are many in the industrial sector who have never "bought in" to the festival and have never attended a play. The reality is that Stratford has been fortunate to have built up a very

York Street, a popular shopping area

successful festival and tourist industry, while at the same time developing an industrial base which has consistently, through depressions and recessions, kept unemployment at one of the lowest levels in Canada.

The dichotomy of Stratford's economy (industry

and tourism) has roots in the city's past. Despite its largely industrial nature, over the years Stratford has developed an increasing awareness of and identity with its English namesake.

Since the 1880s when the city assumed the nickname "The Classic City," the Shakespearean connection has inspired a riverside parks system complete with swans, amateur theatre and music groups, and a Shakespearean gardens. The Stratford Shakespearean Festival Theatre is a culmination of this process of identification.

This illustrated history can only be a selective overview. Many worthy citizens and interesting events could not be included. However, we hope this book will help readers understand how the community evolved into the well-known place it is today. To do this, the book is divided into five chapters followed by a walking tour.

Stratford's city hall, built 1898-99

Chapter one describes the land as the first European settlers found it. It looks at the emergence of the Canada Company with its plans for settlement of the area and its fortuitous decision to create a place named Stratford-on-Avon. It also describes a small organized community ready to take advantage of its coming opportunites.

Chapter two recounts the growth of Stratford as an industrial community before World War I. The arrival of the railway was one of the largest influences on Stratford's development, both industrially and commercially. The railroad's transportation network made Stratford

The Shakespearean Gardens

the ideal location for many important industries. In the later part of this period, Stratford's furniture industry became established. At the same time, there was a growing connection with the Shakespearean name, and by the 1920s Stratford's wonderful parks system was beginning to develop.

Chapter three highlights the city as it was faced with the turmoil of the two World Wars, the Depression and the General Strike of 1933. The furniture industry thrived during the 1920s, thereby helping to shape the economy and the expansion of the community.

Chapter four talks about a new industrial base, which developed after 1950. The city moved away from railway and furniture to a more diversified economy. It was also during this period that the stage was set for the Shakespearean theatre. Tourism has allowed Stratford to become known for its shops, boutiques, heritage buildings and environmental pride.

Chapter five highlights the history of the Stratford Festival including information about the buildings, the productions and other activities.

The walking tour at the end of the book covers the downtown core and the area north of the river. It features many historic sites and buildings that are significant in Stratford's history.

1

THE ORIGINS OF STRATFORD

The origins of Stratford are closely tied to the formation of the Canada Company and its adventures in opening the million-acre Huron Tract from the 1820s to the 1850s. The auspicious naming of Stratford by the company set the stage for the city's identity while events in the first half of the nineteenth century launched the town on the course it follows today.

An Iroquoian village, circa 1500 A.D.

over land bridges, possibly from the south.

Who these first people were is not known, although it is possible that they were the ancestors or relatives of later Algonkian nations such as the Ojibwa, Algonkin, Ottawa or Cree. What we do know is that they were a late Paleolithic or Stone Age People whose survival depended largely on hunting and fishing in the forests and marshlands. Starting about 2,500 years ago, they became part of a trade network that covered a large part of North America.

Eventually, the ancestors of the later Iroquoian nations (Neutral, Huron and Petun) settled in southern Ontario, including Perth County.

An effigy pipe, circa 1500 A.D.

Prehistory

As the glaciers of the last ice age receded, Perth County was part of the first island to emerge from the huge sea that covered much of northeastern North America. Approximately 11,000 years ago the first large animals, along with the first people, arrived

Perth County today, once part of the territory occupied by the historic Neutral

About 1,200 years ago they became agriculturalists living in longhouses in larger and more stable communities. In the early 1600s, when the French under Champlain explored the Great Lakes region, Perth County was considered part of the territory of the Neutral confederation, also called the Attiwandaronk. The immediate area around Stratford was on a high, poorly drained and swampy plain and seems to have been of little interest to the Paleo-Indian since few of their artefacts have been found here. However, just across the county line in Wilmot Township, a very old Paleo-Indian site from about 6,000 years ago and a mid-1400s Neutral site have been excavated.

In the early 1500s, the Neutral concentrated all their villages in a group near Lake Erie. During the 1650s Iroquoian nations in Ontario were destroyed or dispersed by the Five Nations Iroquois confederacy based in what is now upper New York State. For fifty years or so, southwestern Ontario was deserted until the

A prehistoric Neutral pottery vessel, circa 1500 A.D.

Ojibwa and related nations moved back in. It was therefore the Chippewa (Ojibwa) of Sarnia and Kettle Point under Chief Wawanosh who were recognized by the British government as having rights to the area that was to be included in the Huron Tract, established in 1826–27. A preliminary treaty was signed in 1825 followed by a full treaty in 1827 to hand over control of this land to the Crown.

Early historians of Stratford, Robina and Kathleen Lizars, mention in passing an "Indian" campsite in use in the 1840s on the high-school flats at the end of St. Andrew Street. There are no references in the survey notes, surveyor's diaries or other early accounts to native trails and sites or to contact with native peoples in the Stratford area. We do know that they frequented the area after settlement to sell or barter, but we do not know to which group they belonged or from where they came. We can only guess that during the eighteenth and early nineteenth centuries small Ojibwa groups would occasionally have come through the area to hunt.

The Canada Company and the Huron Tract

After the Loyalists arrived in the 1780s, settlement in Upper Canada proceeded very slowly. It became obvious during the War of 1812–1814 with the United States that the thin band of settlers hugging the shores of Lake Ontario and Lake Erie was inadequate for the security of the province.

The largest and most ambitious plan was to found a company of private investors in England to promote settlement, especially of Britain's "surplus" population, in Upper Canada. These people were the rural Scots and English who were displaced by the land

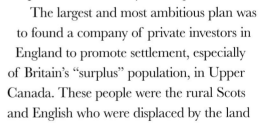

clearances in the Highlands and England and who were considered to be the solid citizens needed for helping the economy of Canada. Artisans from some of the urban centres were also targeted.

The Canada Company was thus founded in London, England, in 1824 on the initiative of Scottish poet John Galt who had spent some time in Canada and was struck by its potential. The company was made up of hundreds of investors interested in the twin objectives of settlement and profit.

The board of directors included individuals who already had connections with Canadian trade and promotion. Hart Logan operated a trading company with offices in Montreal as well as London, England. Edward Ellice was raised in Canada and was a prominent member of the North West Company and the Hudson's Bay Company after the merger of 1821.

Simon McGillivray was from a family who had founded the North West Company in the 1780s, and he had run furs between the West and Montreal himself. His father-in-law was Sir John Easthope. The names of these directors and others were attached to the townships in the Huron Tract a few years later and live on today.

With the support of the British government of the day, the company was incorporated in 1826 and soon had a deal with the government of Upper Canada to take over, at a good price, all of the Crown reserves and half of the clergy reserves. These reserves consisted of about two-sevenths of the lots in every existing township and had been held back for sale at higher prices once the regular five-sevenths of each township's Crown land had been granted or sold. However, since the undeveloped reserves were spread helter-skelter

Perth County Court House and the Avon River

throughout the townships, they were a hindrance to the development of roads and compact communities. The income from the Crown reserves was originally meant for the support of the governor and his staff, and that from the clergy reserves for the maintenance of the clergy. Although the Canada Company did, in accordance with the deal, receive all of the Crown reserves, stiff opposition from Anglican Archdeacon (later Bishop) John Strachan, a member of the executive council, who felt that his Anglican church should get all the proceeds of the clergy reserve fund, prevented the inclusion of the clergy

William "Tiger" Dunlop surveyed much of southwestern Ontario

reserves. In compensation, the Canada Company was given just over a million acres adjacent to Lake Huron, which became known as the Huron Tract.

The company acted quickly by sending John Galt back to Canada to set up an office in York (now Toronto) and to begin settlements in Guelph and Goderich. As soon as these were underway, it was necessary to connect them with a road. The first part of the road from Guelph through Berlin (now Kitchener) to the edge of the Huron Tract (now the eastern end of Perth County) ran through mostly settled areas. From there, however, it was virgin forest for over 100 kilometres.

Doctor William "Tiger" Dunlop who had been hired by Galt as "Warden of the Forests" was in charge of surveying a proof line and establishing a road. Dunlop was a colourful Scot of aristocratic background who loved adventure in the wilds of Canada. He earned his nickname when assigned to rid the Island of Saugur in the Ganges of an infestation of tigers during his tour of duty in India from 1817 to 1820. Setting out to plot a straight line from Punkeydoodle's Corners to Goderich, Dunlop soon realized that this proof line could never become a road because it passed through the middle of the large Ellice Swamp in Ellice Township and another swamp in Logan and McKillop Townships and would have to cross the deep ravines of the Maitland River near Goderich at least twice. Instead, Dunlop and his survey party decided to run a "bridle path" or line of road further to the south to bypass the bends in the river and the large swamps. On July 11, 1827, Dunlop and his party were the first Europeans to arrive at the present site of Stratford, where they spent the night.

When this work was over, Dunlop returned to the mansion overlooking Goderich harbour which he owned with his brother Robert. Considering that people might talk about two bachelors living with a young unmarried housekeeper, Dunlop proposed a toss of the coin to see who would have to marry her. Heads would win, tails lose. Of course Dunlop did not tell his brother that both sides of the coin were heads. After Robert and Louisa were married, Dunlop continued to live in the large house with them (and didn't consider it necessary to move out even after Robert died). Both brothers were elected to the legislature in succession, and Dunlop served as warden of the Huron District as well. He wrote about his experiences and left a famous will, now published many times, in which he made uncomplimentary comments about his brothers and sisters, leaving each an appropriate "gift" while his "dear sister-in-law Louisa" was willed his estate. Dunlop was buried in a specially constructed tomb on his property which is today a historical site.

Fryfogel Inn, built 1844-45

By the summer of 1828, the Huron Road was properly surveyed and hacked out, with corduroy (logs) laid across wet spots. The narrow road through the dense temperate rain forest offered little opportunity to see sunlight, even on the brightest summer day. By the end of the same year, the Company had arranged for three taverns to be built about thirty kilometres apart along this road. These were Fryfogel's, near Shakespeare, which is today a historical site; Seebach's, between Stratford and Mitchell, which is marked by a cairn; and Van Egmond's, between Seaforth and Clinton. For over three years, these were the only points of civilization along the road, as the company sent out John McDonald to survey the tract into townships, and each township into 100-acre lots arranged in rows called "concessions." Improvements to the Huron Road continued. The roadbed was widened and bridges added, including one over the Little Thames, as the Avon River was known at the time. The Little Thames was a creek about a metre wide and about thirty centimetres deep, quite different from the present Avon in summertime.

Conditions at these early taverns were hardly comfortable and at Seebach's sometimes deplorable when supplies of food ran out. Samuel Strickland, brother of pioneer writers Susanna Moodie and Catharine Parr Traill, worked for the Canada Company during this period and, having frequently stayed at these taverns, related a number of experiences in his book, *Twenty-Seven Years in Canada West*.

The construction of the Huron Road and the running of the taverns were the responsibility of Anthony Van Egmond. Apparently connected with the old Dutch family of the famous Count Van Egmond, who had been martyred in the cause of Dutch independence in 1568, Anthony Van Egmond had himself served in the Napoleonic army in the catastrophic Russian campaign, as well as in a Dutch unit against Napoleon at the Battle of Waterloo. His work for the company was paid for in grants of land which included what later became Stratford. Within a few years he had built up many grievances against the company and ran unsuccessfully for the legislature as a Reformer (i.e. Liberal) against Robert Dunlop in 1835 and 1836. Because of his army background, Van Egmond was chosen as the military leader of the Rebellion of 1837. However, the plans went awry and the battle began earlier than scheduled. Van Egmond arrived just in time to be caught and died in jail in Toronto awaiting trial for treason a month later. His family was left with one property in what became the village of Egmondville, where their house is now a museum.

Prominent Stratford resident, John Corry Wilson Daly

The Avon River, once called the Little Thames

The Beginnings of Stratford

Finally in 1832 enough had been surveyed that the company could open the Huron Tract for settlement. To prepare for the expected wave of immigrants, a number of extra taverns or inns were constructed, including one in Stratford. Early in the year William Sargint, an Englishman, was hired to build and operate the new tavern. By this point the Canada Company had already chosen the site near the Little Thames river as the centre of a projected town that would serve the east end of the tract. It seems that the company had also decided that the name of this new town should have a strong English connection as did the two towns it had previously established—Guelph (for the royal family) and Goderich (for the British prime minister.)

The new town was to be named Stratford-upon-Avon after the birthplace of William Shakespeare. The name of the river was changed to the Avon and the company commissioner, Thomas Mercer Jones, presented a portrait of Shakespeare as a signboard for Sargint's new establishment, The Shakespeare Inn. Little did they realize that the name itself would set the stage for future benefits.

The Shakespeare Inn was built in 1832 and destroyed by a fire in 1849. An historical marker is now located adjacent to the site today.

With the inn as its first permanent building, the company proceeded quickly over the next few years to prepare the town site. John Corry Wilson Daly, a wily Irishman, was hired in 1833 to set up a company office here and to contract for and supervise the building and operation of a dam, a grist mill, a sawmill, a

J.C.W. Daly's House, built 1833

store and a distillery. While his house was being built at the head of Ontario Street, Daly made use of two shanties to the west of the bridge that had been left by the road builders a few years earlier.

Daly liked his position of power so well that he appropriated various other official capacities and created a near monopoly. As Canada Company agent he controlled how and when settlers obtained contracts and leases for land in the eastern part of the Huron Tract and was in charge of all of the company's operations. His appointment in 1835 as the sole magistrate (justice of the peace) for the eastern part of the tract meant that he was lawmaker, policeman and judge.

For more than ten years he prevented the appointment of any other magistrates in this area, although there were a dozen or so in the western part of the tract. During this period he was also the postmaster, the only bank manager, and the first district councillor (when democracy finally reached the local level in 1842). Eventually he became the first mayor when Stratford was incorporated as a town, but held the position for only half a year (January to June 1859). The Lizars sisters in their book *In the Days of the*

Canada Company written in Stratford in 1896 aptly called Daly the "little potentate." Daly's sense of control went beyond the grave as well. When he died in 1878, he left his home and property in the centre of Stratford to his three grandsons and their heirs in perpetuity, because he did not trust his son, Thomas Mayne Daly, who was a career politician. When the County of Perth wished to purchase the property for its new courthouse in 1885, it took an act of the Ontario legislature to overturn the will.

As Daly was beginning his work in constructing the core, John McDonald proceeded with a formal survey at the point where the five township plans—North Easthope, South Easthope, Gore of Downie, Downie and Ellice—met. Between 150 and 200 acres were taken from each of these townships and the five township boundary lines became the five main streets of the town—Ontario, Downie, Erie, Huron and Mornington. They would all have met at the main intersection (Ontario and Erie Streets) but adjustments had to be made because of the river and mill pond (now Lake Victoria). This unusual layout of the town, based on five spokes, explains why there is a triangular plaza in the centre of town.

McDonald's plan of 1834 has not survived, but two copies drawn in 1839 still exist. One was Daly's copy to which he added his own names for streets and features, almost all based on his and his wife's families. The other copy from the Canada Company's head office recorded the official street names. These are largely based on British patriotism. One series is for the royal family—Albert, Brunswick, Guelph, Cobourg, Victoria, George; one for the patron saints—St. George, St. Andrew, St. Patrick, St. David; one for the parts of the British Isles in Latin— Britannia (England), Caledonia (Scotland), Hibernia (Ireland), Cambria (Wales).

The Waves of Settlers

In the twenty years following the opening of the Huron Tract for settlement, there were two waves of settlers to the area around Stratford. The first consisted mainly of immigrants from the British Isles and Germany, the countries the Canada Company targeted with advertising. This wave happened to coincide with a general increase in immigration to Canada between 1832 and 1837. The unrest and uncertainty caused by the Depression of 1837 and the rebellions in Upper Canada and Lower

Sebastian Fryfogel, an early settler

Canada during 1837 and 1838 almost completely stopped immigration for a couple of years.

The second wave of settlers followed, peaking in the period between 1842 and 1847, the last year being especially significant because of the famine in Ireland and parts of Europe. Settlers in this second wave came mostly from the same areas as before, often being relatives of those who had arrived ten years earlier. The Scots were mainly from the Lowlands and Perthshire in the Highlands; the Germans mainly from Hesse in central Germany, Hanover in the north, Alsace along the Rhine (now in France) and Bern

Nineteenth-century moulding plane

canton in Switzerland; the Irish mainly from the north, and the English from various areas but especially Cornwall and Devon. This second wave continued into the 1850s and 1860s with immigrants from other areas, most significantly Germans from eastern Europe, Mecklenburg, Prussia, and Saxony, parts of which are now in Poland.

In the late 1840s and early 1850s there was also a large influx of Scots and English who had settled some twenty years earlier in parts of eastern Ontario. These were largely from Lanark County around the town of Perth, and from the Cobourg and Port Hope area of Northumberland County. Further north there was an influx from the southern part of Simcoe County during the 1850s.

These immigrants did not soon leave behind their Old World connections. Most of the groups settled in compact areas concentrated in one township. This was necessary to maintain their churches and languages. Cultural traits were strong and Old World issues continued to influence the settlers, even though these had no relevance to their new home.

The disruption in the Church of Scotland in 1843 over patronage in the state church led to the withdrawal of a significant number of members to form the Free Church of Scotland. St. Andrew's Presbyterian Church in Stratford was not immune to this, even though there was no state church in Canada. In 1844, the minister and some of the members withdrew and formed Knox Presbyterian Church in connection with the Free Church. Both these congregations continue today although the Free Church and the Church of Scotland in Canada reunited in 1875.

In January 1845, a serious riot between the Orange (Protestants) and Green (Catholics) took place in the centre of the village over the results of the election of two district councillors for Downie Township. J.C.W. Daly, who was the incumbent, had announced that he would not run again, but his name was put forward by the Irish Catholics anyway. (Apparently, Daly had changed his mind at the last minute.)

When an Irish Protestant Orangeman won instead of Daly, the Catholic group waited for the victors to emerge from the Shakespeare Tavern and ambushed them. Daly had suspected problems—some claimed he had egged the group on—and had appointed a number of special constables who turned out to be as undisciplined as the rest. Daly sat quietly on his verandah watching the whole incident, and then refused to lay charges. Eventually the matter had to be dealt with by other magistrates from Goderich.

The Growth of a Community

With an ever-increasing population in nearby townships, Stratford became a centre for business and social activity. During the 1830s progress was slow with only a few independent businesses not associated with the Canada Company. The main industry aside from the mills was a foundry set up by John Sharman along Birmingham Street. William Way, a cabinetmaker, came in 1833 and was promptly commissioned by Daly to make him a sofa for his new house. A number of shops, including a store that competed with the company store, and businesses offering the

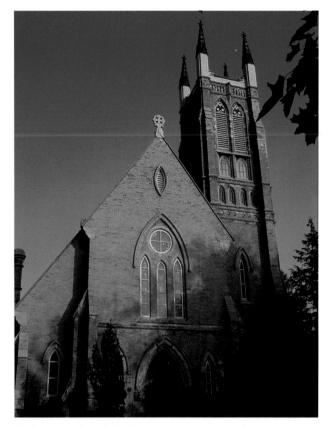

St. James Anglican Church

usual necessities—blacksmith shop, harness maker, cobbler, and so on—were set up.

Social institutions progressed more quickly. A log school was built about 1836 on the corner of Church and St. Andrew Streets and was replaced by a brick school in 1855. The first church was organized in 1838 as St. Andrew's Presbyterian Church with its first frame building erected on St. Andrew Street in 1840. This was followed by St. James Anglican Church organized in 1840 with a church built on land set aside by the Canada Company along St. George Street, now part of Mornington Street. The Catholics were organized as St. Joseph's Church about 1840 and built a church on Huron Street in 1844. All of these denominations, as well as the Lutherans who had organized two congregations outside Stratford in 1835, had been served since 1832 by occasional missionary visits. In the mid-forties Knox Presbyterian Church, the Wesleyan Methodist Church and the Congregational Church were built. The Evangelical Association (German Methodist) established a mission field just east and west of Stratford in 1840.

The 1840s and 1850s saw a much more rapid increase in the rural population and therefore a need for many more services and businesses. Although the focus was on serving the largely rural community, some urban services and small industries also developed. Stratford became a bustling village and an important urban centre. Initially all the buildings were frame. As the town became more prosperous, merchants and wealthier people could afford brick structures. The most common style in the 1850s was the Regency cottage. This cottage was a one and a half storey building with a flat, hipped roof, a centre hall plan and sidelight and transom windows. Local orange-red brick was used and wealthier families added embellishments such as contrasting brick decoration. Many of these cottages still exist, especially in older neighbourhoods like Mornington, Britannia and St. David Streets.

Horseshoe and cobblers' mould, circa 1850

Wood and leather chisels, circa 1850

In 1848, most of the houses in the rural community around Stratford were log although there were only nine such houses in Stratford. Working-class people lived in frame houses until the 1870s when the affluence brought by the railroad made brick buildings affordable to everyone.

Social organizations were also formed for a variety of activities. The most important was the Stratford Agricultural Society, which has organized an annual fair and other events every year since its founding in 1841.

The Mechanics Institute was formed in 1846 by tradesmen to provide a library for its members. At first the books were largely trade-oriented but a general library open to anyone who wished to join soon developed. The Mechanics Institute became the public library in the 1890s.

Most organized leisure activities were only available for the wealthier families who had the time. The boat club was formed in 1845 by some of these families. The story is that there was one boat on the Avon River which was used by all members. The club existed until the boat deteriorated and the members became too old to be active. The same families also participated in lawn bowling, cricket and curling.

An Independent Municipality

As people settled in the townships around Stratford and in the town site, local government was established in the area. Before 1850, local government everywhere in Upper Canada was largely non-democratic, controlled by the magistrates meeting in the District Court of General Sessions. The magistrates legislated regulations throughout the districts and called for meetings of the township ratepayers. These meetings, dealing with the control of fences and stray animals and with the maintenance of local roads, were the only very limited, form of democracy. During this period, Stratford was divided among the four townships—North Easthope, South Easthope, Ellice and Downie—and had no separate status.

Regency cottages, like this one, were popular in the 1850s

Until 1841 these townships were part of the London District, centred on the town of London. The district magistrates took little notice of settlement in the Stratford area, which was hardly accessible to them, and neglected to call township meetings in the area until 1836. Matters were not much better when the Huron District, consisting of the Huron Tract townships, was created in October 1841. The centre was now at Goderich which was no closer to Stratford, although it was more accessible by road. However, with the beginning of 1842 a new District Council directly elected by the township meetings was established. This introduced a somewhat larger measure of democracy as legislating regulations was transferred from the magistrates to an elected council.

Soon agitation began to turn the east end of the Huron Tract into a separate district. J. C. W. Daly and his archrival, J. J. E. Linton, set about to build support for this new "District of Peel." The proposal was presented to the provincial legislature in 1847, but was delayed when elections were called. These resulted in a Reform (i.e. Liberal) majority, and other priorities took over. The new government decided on abolishing the districts and replacing them with smaller counties. So Daly and Linton pushed their plan successfully for a new county. Linton chose the name "Perth" for the county because of the many settlers in the area from Perthshire, Scotland.

Linton himself was a Scottish immigrant who had settled in Downie Township in 1833. Finding farming not to his liking, he and his wife moved in with her relatives along the Huron Road in North Easthope Township a year later and set up two schools. By 1836, he moved into Stratford so that he could keep an eye on J. C. W. Daly. Soon he was involved as secretary in the formation of St. Andrew's Church and then the

Agricultural Society. He secured an appointment as a notary public and a coroner, but was prevented from becoming a magistrate by Daly's influence. After his role in the formation of Perth County, Linton never let the county forget its debt to him. An abolitionist and a great moralist, he persuaded the county to pass a morals bylaw (and subsequent amendments) even though this was beyond the powers of a county government. As a result of this bylaw, one could spend twenty days in jail for playing marbles on Sunday.

Perth County came into being in January, 1850 with Stratford as the county seat. Before it could separate completely from Huron County, the councillors had to build a courthouse and jail in Stratford. After opposition to the idea in 1850, the council decided to go ahead a year later. The buildings were completed in January, 1853. As centre of a new county, Stratford developed a new sense of importance and at the beginning of the next year, 1854, it was incorporated as a village separate from the surrounding townships.

St. Andrew's Presbyterian Church, circa 1910

2

THE CLASSIC CITY

The second half of the nineteenth century saw the growth of Stratford's prosperity as the community established itself as a railway hub and an industrial centre. It was during this period that many of Stratford's landmarks such as the courthouse and the city hall were built.

The Railway Arrives

The main excitement in the new village in the 1850s was the arrival of the railway, an event which would shape the economic prosperity of Stratford for the next hundred years. And it wasn't just one, but two railways that were coming. The railway vastly improved transportation for people and goods, thereby opening access to much larger markets, which was a great benefit for the community. The railway also encouraged

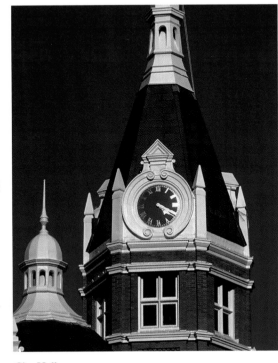

City Hall

more industries and businesses to centralize.

A trip to Toronto that took about three days before the arrival of the railway could now be done in four hours. Mail and newspapers from Toronto could be delivered the same day, assuring much quicker communication with the outside world.

The first line to arrive in October, 1856, was the Grand Trunk Railway (GTR) from Toronto. It had started as the Toronto and Goderich Railway Company in 1847, renamed four years later as the Toronto and Guelph Railway Company. By 1853, this company had become involved in a larger plan for a trunk line through the province from Montreal to Sarnia and Chicago. Together with two other railway companies along this line, it was absorbed by the

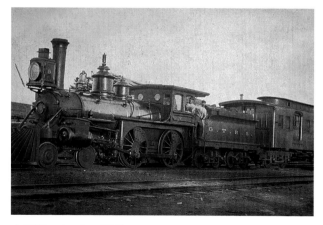

A GTR train, circa 1880

new Grand Trunk Railway. The originally projected terminus at Goderich was changed to Sarnia and the whole line was completed in 1860.

In December, 1856, only two months after the completion of the Grand Trunk line from Toronto, the first train on the Buffalo and Lake Huron Railway arrived in Stratford. It would have arrived much earlier if it had not been for the financial difficulties of the Buffalo, Brantford and Goderich Railway Company, founded in 1851, which became insolvent in mid-1855 after much of the roadbed and track had already been laid.

The Village of Stratford and the County of Perth had invested heavily in the company. However, the reeve of Stratford, Alexander Barrington Orr, had been

A physical examination book for GTR employees

A GTR dining car lamp, circa 1890

warned of the impending problem and made sure that the village got its money out. He was also a member of the county council, but did not pass on the information to the county. The county was burdened with this bad debt for many years afterward. Within weeks a new company, the Buffalo and Lake Huron Railway Company, was incorporated to purchase the rights of the bankrupt railway and proceed with the line. It was finally completed to Goderich in 1858.

The crossing of two railway lines made Stratford a hub and soon the railways were trying to coordinate their services. This effort culminated in a large, frame Union Station on the corner of Guelph and Downie Streets, which opened in 1870. In the meantime, the Grand Trunk Railway took over control of the Buffalo and Lake Huron line. With both lines under the control of the GTR, Stratford became a major competitor as the site for new locomotive repair shops. But the choice was not based solely on merit.

When T. H. Roberts, the GTR superintendent, arrived in town to view the prospective site, Mayor Thomas Mayne Daly took him home to dinner. Daly's daughter Sarah, who was also at dinner, seems to have made quite an impression on Roberts. Roberts had found a wife, and the shops came to Stratford.

Almost overnight the population exploded with the arrival of over 300 skilled workmen and their families. Houses were in very short supply and many lived for quite a while in tents on railway lands. This resulted in a housing boom which introduced Ontario cottages, mostly built near the train station and the GTR

GTR shops, showing 1879 addition

shops. Hotels were built, including two opposite the train station. Other nearby buildings were also used for hotels. The locomotive shops expanded in 1889 and 1907, resulting in further population booms and an increase in workers' houses throughout Stratford. The shop buildings still stand near the corner of Downie and Patrick Streets. Land adjacent to the shops is now a municipal parking lot.

Local 103 of the International Association of Machinists (IAM), the first local in Canada, was formed at the shops in 1890. The IAM quickly became a force in the railway industry and the machinists soon had the best wages and benefits. The shops were perceived as the best place in town to work.

Two more railways arrived in Stratford shortly after the shops opened—the Port Dover and Lake Huron (from the south in 1875) and the Stratford and Huron (to the north in 1877). By 1881 they had also been absorbed by the GTR.

The interior of the GTR shops, circa 1890

Young Tom Edison

The most famous employee of the Grand Trunk Railway in Stratford was Thomas Alva Edison. In 1863, aged sixteen, Edison obtained his first job at the Stratford train station as a night telegraph operator. He apparently lived at the Albion Hotel and frequently visited with Thomas Winter who operated a telegraph office next door. Later stories from the Winter family tell of Edison's interest in inventing and their concern that he might blow up the hotel.

Thomas Alva Edison

the American West before becoming a world-famous inventor. Years later the GTR presented Edison's last pay cheque of $28 to his father in a ceremony at Port Huron.

In 1940, with the making of *Young Tom Edison*, Stratford was chosen as one of three locations for an official premiere of the movie. Actor Mickey Rooney was invited to attend but could not because of his premieres in Detroit and Port Huron. He sent an autographed picture with his regrets to Mayor Thomas Henry. A plaque commemorating Edison's time in Stratford was placed in the railway station as part of the celebrations.

Edison's fertile mind was already at work in Stratford, long before he invented the light bulb. At the train station he invented a clock device attached to the telegraph which sent a signal each half-hour to his supervisor. In this way he could sleep on the job and have time to experiment during the day. The regularity of the device made the supervisor suspicious, and he was soon found out.

After six or seven months Edison almost caused a collision between two trains at the junction. One train went through the switch and was derailed, while the other managed to stop just in time. Not waiting to be fired, he quickly made his way back home to Port Huron, Michigan and then spent a few years drifting in

First Town Hall and the New Core Area

The Canada Company had originally expected that the focal point of the new settlement would be the mill pond and that development would proceed north and south from the river along Huron and Ontario Streets. This focus changed when the railways laid their lines and built their stations further to the south, near the edge of the town plan. The town hall was built in a new market square, closer to the railway, and the centre of town shifted to Wellington and Downie Streets and Market Place.

The money recouped by the village of Stratford from the Buffalo, Brantford and Goderich railway collapse provided the community with funds to build a town hall in 1857. The town hall was an ambitious undertaking for a community of two thousand people, but it reflected a confidence in Stratford's future prosperity. Toronto architect William Thomas was hired to build a neoclassical structure, which included four stores at street level and a council chamber and offices above. At the back there was a market arcade facing Market Place and an auditorium for 1,600 people upstairs. The building was also known as the Market Building because the original agreement with former owner, Donald McDonald, required that the area be used for an open market and not built on. When the building was constructed, no one was sure how the McDonald family would accept the change, but no legal action was taken and the building stood until 1897, when it was destroyed by fire.

Stratford's first town hall, circa 1870

The first brick block in Stratford was the Mill Block along Ontario Street with the Peter Wood's Albion Hotel built in 1855 at its east end. Built in the neoclassical style, the Albion Hotel became an important site for public meetings when other buildings were not yet completed. The first brick commercial building was located on the south side of Ontario Street across from the hotel. It was owned by Peter Robinson Jarvis, a prominent tea merchant, and was built in 1857. All that remains of this building today are two additions from the 1860s.

Over the next two decades the frame buildings that had dominated the downtown area were slowly replaced by brick buildings. Until the building boom of the 1880s and 1890s, the streetscape remained an amalgam of brick and frame.

With a growing population and prosperity, Stratford was incorporated as a town in 1859 and was divided into five wards with Shakespearean names: Avon, Falstaff, Hamlet, Shakespeare and Romeo. Although a few streets were also given Shakespearean names in early surveys, the ward names (which are still in use today) had a major influence on the community's connection with Shakespeare. The nearby village of Bell's Corners had changed its name to Shakespeare at a public meeting in 1852 at the request of the post office department. Shakespeare was successfully promoted and today is known for its antiques trade.

In 1857, when Stratford built the Northern Gravel Road through the Ellice Swamp to the grain farms of Mornington Township, a small village developed along the road and was named Gadshill.

(Gadshill is Falstaff's home in Shakespeare's *Henry IV*). Unlike the village of Shakespeare, Gadshill has not had the fortune of being located on a major tourist highway into Stratford and remains a rural residential village.

In 1864, the whole town took advantage of the 300th anniversary of Shakespeare's birth to hold a special tercentenary celebration that was well-attended despite the rain. An oak tree commemorating the anniversary was planted in Shakespeare Place next to the location of the original Shakespeare Tavern. Other festivities, including a dance, followed the tree-planting ceremony. The tree was later cut down when a post office was built, and the site is now Memorial Park. Shakespeare's birthday continues to be celebrated each year.

The most alarming event during this early period was the Fenian Raids, cross-border attacks on Canada by members of the Fenian Irish Republican Brotherhood (a forerunner of the IRA) who resided in the United States. These attacks occurred between 1866 and 1870 shortly after the U.S. Civil War and the Trent Affair which almost caused the United States to declare war on the British and Canada. These tensions were the most immediate reason for the British North American colonies to form the new Dominion of Canada on July 1, 1867, an event well celebrated in Stratford then and every year since. During the raids (which luckily

The Shakespeare Tercentenary, 1864

never reached Stratford), the town hall was converted into barracks for British regular soldiers. The provincial government recognized various volunteer units as reinforcements rather than relying on the compulsory "sedentary" militia which by then had become a farce. The two companies in Stratford, the Volunteer Rifle Company and the Infantry, were both mobilized to serve on the fronts in Windsor and Niagara. This meant that a lot of the men from the area left Stratford, with the numbers mobilized as significant as in both of the World Wars.

On September 14, 1866, these two companies and two others in the county were organized as the 28th (Perth) Battalion of Infantry. During the Boer War in 1900, the battalion became the 28th Perth Regiment, subsequently dropping the number from its name.

With the sudden increase in population caused by the locomotive shops, the town was in need of more schools. A change in Ontario's education legislation coincided closely with this development. There had been one common or elementary school, one separate school and one grammar or high school before 1870. In quick succession five elementary schools were opened in the early 1870s and, in keeping with Stratford's identity, were named after each Shakespearean ward. The original public school became Central Public School and was eventually closed in 1915.

All of the later public schools also received Shakespearean names. The original schools—Romeo, Shakespeare, Hamlet, Falstaff and Avon—have now been joined by Juliet, Anne Hathaway, Portia, Bedford and King Lear. This naming process was not adopted by the high schools or the Catholic schools.

A second separate school was built in the 1870s beside the new Loretto Academy, a private Catholic high school. Both schools were taught by the Loretto Sisters who also had a convent in Stratford. By the late 1890s the original separate school beside the church was closed. The old grammar school built in 1853 on Norman Street was replaced by the collegiate on St. Andrew Street in 1879. The privately run Central Business College also operated in Stratford from 1887 to the 1950s and was at one time the largest such school in southwestern Ontario.

Romeo School, circa 1912

Stratford Becomes a City

In the early 1880s, the town began to aspire to a grander image. One cause for concern, however, was a threat that the County of Perth, of which Stratford was a part, would hold a referendum on banning liquor. Afraid that such a vote would result in problems for the city's prosperity—there were quite a few licensed hotels, as well as two breweries—the town requested special legislation from the provincial government to incorporate Stratford as a city separate from the county, despite having well below the 15,000

people needed. On March 31, 1885, Stratford became a city. At the time of the formal celebration held in July, the question of a suitable nickname was raised in the local press with numerous letters in reply. Finally, a suggestion by prominent merchant James Corcoran to call Stratford "The Classic City" ended the debate. It would seem that in the 1880s the residents of Stratford could already identify with the literary heritage associated with the city's name. The nickname was frequently used over the next seventy years until it was replaced by "The Festival City."

The incorporation as a city occurred just as Stratford was moving into a period of industrial expansion that lasted into the 1920s. With rail transportation readily available in six directions and Stratford's location in the centre of southwestern Ontario, industry had good access to markets across North America. This encouraged existing industries to expand operations and new industries to establish themselves here.

The largest of these industries was furniture. Beginning with a few individual cabinetmakers and small planing mills in the early years, the furniture industry started to develop when the Porteous and McLagan factory was established in 1885. George McLagan had apprenticed with Stratford cabinetmakers Campbell and Graham before moving to Grand

Rapids, Michigan, the centre of American furniture making, to improve his skills in fine furniture design. It was there that he also became familiar with a factory system of production. After a number of years, he returned to Stratford and was able to enter a partnership with Robert Porteous who had been operating a small business. With the design abilities of McLagan, the new company started to produce fine furniture in various styles for parlours, halls and dining rooms. Most of the furniture was made of oak and mahogany, but walnut was also used during periods when it was popular. The firm quickly established a Canada-wide reputation. After Porteous retired in 1898 and a catastrophic fire destroyed the downtown factory in 1900, McLagan established a new course for the industry by building the first of the large brick factories in the east end, which was to become Stratford's furniture district. The factory on Trinity and Douro Streets had expanded greatly by the time of McLagan's death in 1918. It had been joined by seven other furniture companies.

Thomas Orr and Son was the most successful among the more traditional furniture producers, all of whom had disappeared by the early 1900s. In 1885, Orr expanded his planing mill beside his home on Cobourg Street, to produce sideboards. After his son Joseph sold the factory in 1901, it was soon purchased by the parks board as a link in the parks system along the river. The family home at 50 Cobourg Street, now the offices of Orr Insurance, is one of Stratford's heritage buildings.

During the late 1800s,

Stratford was also known for the production of agricultural implements. The factories producing these implements were joined in the early 1900s by a number of textile mills, but neither of these industries had a national impact.

Public works developed slowly with board sidewalks along the streets starting in the 1850s. The first coal-oil streetlights were installed in 1864, fuelled by gas in the 1870s and electricity in 1888. The gasworks built in 1875 by the Stratford Gas Company was taken over by the Public Utilities Commission in 1928. The waterworks, built in 1883 by the Stratford Water Supply Company, was transferred to the Water Commission in 1904. Electricity was brought into the city in 1887 and was taken over by the Light and Heat Commission in 1910. The two public commissions were merged into the Stratford Public Utilities Commission in 1915.

The first sewers were installed in 1885 and the first treatment plant was built in 1900. Finally, about 1900, the city became serious about paving streets, and the old moniker "Muddy Stratford" was no longer justified.

Most of the downtown buildings that survive today date from the 1880s to 1900 and bear the names of the merchants and hotelkeepers who built them. Owners of adjacent buildings agreed on a similar design to create continuity on the streetscape. Many of the brick buildings began as two storeys with the third storey added later. The tin cornices and soffits which adorn many of the buildings were made by the artisans of the Grand Trunk Railway. These features, as well as the decorative lintels and brickwork, identify these buildings as Victorian. (More information about these buildings and other core buildings is included in the walking tour.)

Stratford's continued prosperity and commercial growth provided the need and the finances to build some new public buildings in the core, including the post office in 1884, the fire hall in 1895, the library in 1902 and the armouries in 1905. All of these were prominent buildings.

The library was one of the first Carnegie Libraries in Canada. Because of the opposition to the use of Andrew Carnegie's money, his name never appeared on the building and there was no opening ceremony. Originally the library faced St. Andrew Street, until an addition in 1926 when the present front was added.

Two prominent landmarks of national significance were also constructed in the core during this period— the Perth County Court House and the new Stratford City Hall. Within five years of completion, the first county buildings did not meet the standards of the provincial government. Furthermore, the county magistrates refused to hold court in the courthouse because of the smell from the jail immediately behind it. For over twenty years, the county council fought with the province over having to replace the buildings. However, the county eventually obtained suitable land, and London architect George F. Durand was hired to design a new courthouse and jail in the Queen Anne revival or high Victorian style. Characteristics of the style include bichromal brick, the borrowing of architectural features from other styles and the use of many windows and multi-decorative chimneys. The courthouse, built between 1885–1887, features numerous wall vents and has fireplaces in almost every office. Durand autographed or signed the building and was criticized by his colleagues for acting like an artist, not an architect. The building can be seen for at least two miles as you approach Stratford from the east. It remains an

Stratford's Post Office, circa 1880

important landmark downtown and its majestic presence suggests a prosperous county that took pride in its administrative building.

Durand's design for the jail matched that of the courthouse. This time, it was built half a block away from the courthouse so that it could not disrupt court again. In 1910, a new registry office was built by local architect T. J. Hepburn, who was asked to match the Victorian flavour of the other county buildings.

Following the destruction of the old town hall by fire in 1897, a plebiscite was held with the option to accept plans to rebuild the town hall, as submitted by architect Alexander Hepburn. The other option was to accept plans for a new building as submitted by Toronto architect George W. King. King's plans won and the new foundation was laid with a cornerstone ceremony held on November 2, 1898.

The city council members of the time commissioned local stonecutter James Gadsby to make a tablet for the foyer of the building that would list their names as well as those of the architects and builders. A dispute occurred between the architects when one of them, James Siddall, saw that he was listed as an "ASS" architect. There was a spot for one more letter, but the dispute was whether the letter should signify an assistant or associate. This issue never was resolved. Largely because of this dispute, the tablet was not hung in the foyer until 1974.

The growth of the railway allowed for the money to build houses for labourers and the wealthier people. Gothic houses became prominent from the 1870s to the 1890s. These included Ontario cottages which were built near the railroad and were considered the first brick homes owned by labourers. Thus they became known as a working man's cottage. Similar to the Regency cottage in height and with a centre hall plan, these houses featured a gable and window over the door and an extra half storey for additional living space. Many of these local buff-coloured brick houses still stand, and some retain original details like the decorative gingerbread or wood trim.

Larger Gothic buildings like the Ontario house and triple-gabled buildings were owned by the supervisors and businessmen of Stratford. The Ontario house was identical to the cottage except that it had one and

three-quarter storeys instead of one and a half. Triple-gabled houses featured decorated gables on the front façade of the building and were also one and three-quarters storeys in height. All of these building styles could have gingerbread, making them look more ornate and expensive.

Larger Italianate homes became popular during the 1880s, especially for businessmen and wealthier residents. These houses were two storeys in height and asymmetrical in shape. The identifying features were the ornate brackets that were located underneath the eaves and on the rounded one or two storey bay windows. Matching brackets also adorned the bay soffits.

Also popular in the late 1890s was the Queen Anne revival style, used for the homes of the more affluent families in Stratford. Apart from the other characteristics mentioned with the courthouse, key identifying features of Queen Anne revival style buildings were the broken roof line, the two to two and a half storey structure and the use of contrasting bricks,

Ontario houses, like this one, were popular in the nineteenth century

textures and colours. These houses were perfect for people with money because they could be very ostentatious, allowing the wealthy a way to show off.

As Stratford grew, it became necessary to accom-

An Italianate house with a neoclassical portico

modate more people. What is interesting is that there are no areas in Stratford with uniquely old-style houses. Originally, the town lots were about one-quarter of an acre. When the railway first came, Gothic Ontario cottages and houses could be located on these lots. Around the turn of the century, these lots were subdivided and newer homes built, usually closer to the street.

During the 1880s, a social movement spearheaded by a local women's group, with authors Robina and Kathleen Lizars as the leaders, examined many social

issues that affected Stratford. Up until this time there had been no publicly funded hospital; people who were ill and had nowhere to go were brought before a magistrate or justice of the peace and sent to the local jail. Inspectors' reports mention the lack of criminals and the number of vagrant and sick people in the jail. If found guilty under the Vagrancy Act, people were sentenced to hard labour.

The Lizars sisters felt that the county and city should be providing people with better options. They also felt the sick and destitute should not be imprisoned with criminals.

As a result, a city hospital was suggested as the Golden Jubilee project in Stratford and the County of Perth. However, it was not until 1891 that the hospital was finally built. It was designed by George F. Durand, the London architect who also designed the court-

Stratford's general hospital, circa 1910

house, jail and pumping station. The official opening of the debt-free hospital was held in May, 1891. Throughout the years, many changes occurred to the building, but it functioned as a hospital until the 1950s.

The House of Refuge was not built until 1897. It provided care for the elderly and the destitute. All able-bodied residents were required to work in the fields belonging to the home. It was sponsored by the County of Perth with financial contributions from the city of Stratford, surrounding townships and the town of St. Marys.

In 1904, Stratford residents began to express concern about Queen's Park, which was overgrown and untended, and about the threat of the Canadian Pacific Railway line along the riverbank. In response, the city council established the Stratford Parks Board to operate a unified parks system. In 1871, Avondale Cemetery had been opened and treated like a park, but bequests of land from William Battershall, R. Thomas Orr and others also required an organized system. Frederick G. Todd, a landscape architect from Montreal, was hired to design the parks system, especially Upper Queen's Park.

In 1900, the provincial government began to look for locations to build four more normal schools. In 1906, Stratford enticed the government to look at Stratford by offering any site within the city's limits for free. The site chosen was Upper Queen's Park. Initially, the newly formed parks board was opposed to this location because they felt it would interfere with Todd's design. Eventually a compromise was reached that allowed the building to be constructed and the landscaping to remain in keeping with the surrounding park area. Another altercation occurred in 1913 when the provincial government wanted to fence in the school yard. The parks board was adamant that this was not acceptable, since the original agreement approved the site as a park area. The building opened in 1908, even though it was not quite finished inside, and operated as a teachers' college until 1973.

By World War I, Stratford had grown into a thriving city. Its increasing prosperity could be seen in the preponderance of brick buildings where only frame ones had stood earlier. Because of its location, it had become a railway hub and benefitted greatly from the GTR locomotive shops, which employed about half the people in the town. The furniture industry had also emerged as a major force in the economy and a new civic pride had led to the formation of a parks system, which was to play an important role in Stratford's later development.

A boat regatta on the Avon River, circa 1890.

3

War and Peace

The first half of the twentieth century witnessed three major disruptions to life in Stratford and elsewhere in the world—the two World Wars and the Depression. But it also saw one of the most prosperous periods in the city's history during the 1920s when the railway and furniture industries reached their peaks. Despite these ups and downs, the community continued to develop its parks system and became known for its hockey teams and music festival.

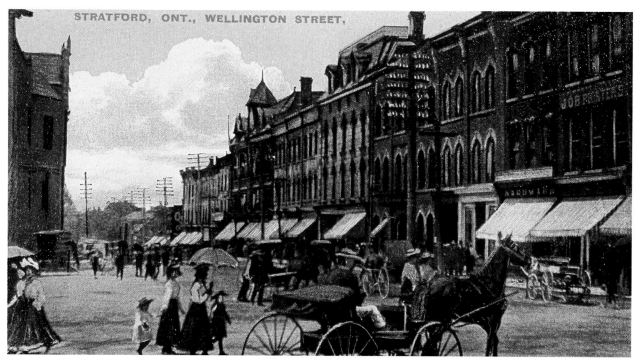

Wellington Street, circa 1910

The Great War

During World War I, the existing militia units, including the Perth Regiment, were bypassed and new battalions drawn from larger areas. Most of the men recruited in 1914 were in the First Battalion, Canadian Expeditionary Force (CEF) or the Eighteenth Battalion (CEF), in Southwestern Ontario. From 1915 to 1917 the 100th Battalion was recruited in Perth County, but the men were distributed to other battalions to fight or sent to the Eighth Reserve Battalion. The Perth Regiment was subsequently awarded battle honours for the Battles of Ypres and Festubert.

This was the first war in which Canada participated under separate command from the British services. At the end of 1917, conscription was implemented but few of the conscripts actually reached the front before the war ended on November 11, 1918. The returning soldiers brought back with them the tragic flu epidemic of 1918–1919.

Almost every ablebodied man in Stratford enlisted to fight during the war. As in other communities, the residents of Stratford tried to continue leading normal lives despite the situation in Europe and the potential for losing loved ones. Local newspaper accounts are full of day-to-day reports about the war, local men killed in action and how Stratford was keeping its morale high with patriotic celebrations and fundraising events.

GTR Station, 1913

Three hundred and forty-five men from Stratford and vicinity were killed in World War I—a significant loss for the community. Following the war, the veterans, with the help of the Imperial Order of the Daughters of the Empire, proposed a monument to commemorate the dead. Eventually, renowned Canadian sculptor Walter S. Allward was commissioned to design a memorial. Allward chose the classic theme of right versus might.

Industrial Expansion

The first decades of the twentieth century saw the rapid expansion of industry in Stratford. In 1923, the Grand Trunk Railway was amalgamated with other railways to form the publicly owned Canadian National Railway. The railway's apprenticeship program, started in 1908, continued to flourish. Young men from the local area and farther away learned drafting, mathematics and other specialized courses for the operation and design of engines. Many of these men continued to work at the shops until they retired. In 1949, following a major expansion, the shops were able to accommodate more repairs of the larger new engines.

Following World War I, an economic boom had a positive effect on Stratford's industries. Like the railway, the furniture industry reached its peak during the

1920s. A summary in the *Financial Post* on April 26, 1929, noted that Stratford's thirteen furniture companies were among the largest in the country and accounted for "nearly one-sixth of the total output of furniture in Canada." The wages paid out represented almost 14 percent of the total for all furniture companies in the country. Stratford employed 1,300 of the 11,000 workers in this industry across Canada.

A whole range of furniture was made in Stratford and shipped to dealers all over North America. McLagan was well known for fine dining room and living room

A phonograph, post 1910

furniture, but it expanded into bedroom suites as well. McLagan Phonograph Ltd. emerged as its own company in 1916 to continue as the largest maker of radio and phonograph cabinets in Canada. The Stratford Chair Company was formed in 1904, but soon became a McLagan subsidiary. It specialized in chairs and more moderately priced furniture. There were many other furniture companies: Globe Wernicke, later Preston-Noelting, which produced office furniture and stationery; Farquharson-Gifford, which specialized in

upholstered chesterfields and easy chairs; Imperial Rattan; the Stratford Manufacturing Company; and later Moore-Bell and Kroehler.

The companies worked well together to promote "Made in Stratford" shows and international trade shows, which were held regularly from the early 1900s to the 1930s. Each company was also directly connected to the rail system for easy shipping of products across the continent.

The rapid expansion of these factories up to and through the 1920s led to about a 40 percent growth in Stratford's population. The new people were coming largely from the rural areas around Stratford and from other cities in the southern part of the province. However, the city also received its share of the wave of immigrants from large English cities. Quite a number of these were skilled tradespeople who found work at the furniture factories or the CNR shops soon after arriving.

This influx resulted in a building boom featuring rows of Queen Anne box-style homes. These two to two and a half storey houses featured a box-like shape

A McLagan sideboard, circa 1930

Stratford, looking north to Huron Street, circa 1910

and an A-shaped gable with cedar shakes that looked like fish scales. Larger than the earlier Ontario cottages, these working-class houses were built using copybook designs that had begun with the Queen Anne revival style. Copybooks provided specifications for developers and contractors. As a result, many neighbourhoods feature several Queen Anne box homes, some of which have reversed floor plans to allow for variation in the design.

The Depression

The boom years did not last long. The American stock market crash of 1929 affected all global markets and resulted in an economic depression throughout the world. The Depression of the 1930s affected Stratford as it did many other communities. Production, job security and wages fell. These factors led to strains in labour relations, just at a time when organizers from the Workers' Unity League (WUL) arrived in the city in 1933. They had successfully set

The court house and Dufton woollen mills, circa 1910

1933 general strike

McLagan furniture workers on strike, 1933

military was requested during a strike in Canada.

Preston-Noelting settled on October 18, and the rest followed between November 3 and 8. The settlements improved working conditions and resulted in modest pay increases. Only one person was arrested, but the police chief was forced to resign and the mayor stepped down. Alderman O. J. Kerr, one of the leaders of the strike, was elected mayor along with six (of ten) aldermen from the labour movement.

As the Depression continued, the City of Stratford had to find money to pay for direct relief and for unemployment relief. Industrial employees were laid off, but some took wage cuts to ensure fellow workers remained employed. Despite some layoffs, the strength of the railway unions ensured that the railway employees only took a 5 percent cut in wages.

up locals of furniture workers in Toronto and had chosen Stratford as their next target. Within a month, they had organized six of the seven factories and provided the managers with the workers' demands. On September 15, 1933 these workers went out on strike.

Once the furniture strike had started, the WUL was also successful in organizing employees at Swift's as members of the Food Workers' Industrial Union. The women went on strike on September 21 followed a few days later by the men. An incident at Swift's led Mayor Graff to ask for military reinforcements. The soldiers arrived by train, followed by four Carden-Lloyd machine gun carriers. Although these reinforcements were never used, much indignation arose over the show of force and this was the last time that the

Social Activities

One of the most important ways Stratford residents raised their spirits during the Depression was through sports. Stratford has always been known for its sports teams, beginning in the early years with cricket, lacrosse, baseball and curling. Boating and bicycling were also favourite pastimes.

During the 1930s, Stratford became known as "the hockey town" because of the calibre of hockey players and teams that it produced. The Senior A Champions, the Indians (later the Kroehler's team), were always at the top of their league. Similarly, the Junior B Cullitons team continues to top its league. These teams have been the training grounds for NHL players.

One of the most popular and famous players to come from the town was Howie Morenz, the "Stratford Streak." Born in 1902 in Mitchell, Ontario, he moved with his family in 1914 to Stratford where he played hockey. In 1923, he signed with the Montreal Canadiens where he played for all but two seasons and became one of the greatest hockey legends of all time. In January, 1937, Morenz was slammed into the boards during a bodycheck and broke his leg in five places. His career was over. Demoralized, he died in November, 1937, from a heart attack. A floral tribute in the shape of a number 7 was placed on the coffin,

Stratford's hockey team, including Howie Morenz, 1923

and the Montreal Canadiens retired his number. On March 9, 1938, a local tribute was held for Morenz before a game when former teammate Walter "Butch" Kelterborn placed a floral wreath on crossed hockey sticks.

Harness racing and skating were also important to Stratford from the Depression era on. Harness racing was so popular that meets were held for two to three days during the July 1 holiday. Interest in the sport declined during the war years before rising again in the 1950s. Harness racing is no longer an active sport in Stratford, although many excellent race horses are raised in the surrounding area.

The Stratford Skating Club was formed in 1937 and went through several name changes. One of the club's successes was Donald McPherson, who won the Men's World Championship in 1963. The skating club continues to be active today.

In 1932, the Lion's Club sponsored a public swimming pool adjacent to the swimming area on the Avon River. As well as being a safer and cleaner alternative than the polluted Avon, the pool provided children with the opportunity to learn how to swim.

QUEEN VICTORIA LAKE AND LION'S SWIMMING POOL, STRATFORD, ONT., CANADA.

Victoria Lake pergola and Lion's Pool, circa 1935

The Arts

Theatres, like Stratford's Theatre Albert, were popular from the turn of the century through to the 1950s. While many theatres were built for live performances, by the 1930s the trend soon turned to movies. At one time, Stratford had three movie theatres. They were the Theatre Albert, which became the Griffin, the Majestic, and finally the Avon; the Princess; and the Classic, which later became the Vogue.

Dramatic productions were provided regularly by various local groups, among them the Tamarue Players (later the Little Theatre) in the 1920s, the Temple Choir of the Masonic Lodge which presented an annual Gilbert and Sullivan operetta, and the Shakespearean Society of the normal school which performed a number of plays each year.

In the 1920s when there was very little professional theatre in Canada, Stratford citizens already seemed to take pride in living up to their nickname through local theatre and music.

Stratford was lucky to have many talented music teachers and musicians in the area. These included organist and composer Henry Easun and piano and voice teachers Cora B. Ahrens, Ida Kollman, W. B. Bothwell and Florence Polley. Cora B. Ahrens published many books about teaching children how to sing. Some of these are still widely used today. In 1927, a music festival was begun at the suggestion of Bothwell, who was the music teacher at the normal school. Originally sponsored by the Perth County Music Teachers' Federation, the festival has been sponsored by the Kiwanis Club since the 1950s and is one of the oldest music festivals in Ontario. Various groups have provided musical entertainment at regular intervals including the CNR band, the Stratford Boys Band, the Perth Regiment band and the Alpha Choristers.

Often this musical entertainment would be held in the bandshell, located on Lakeside Dr. This bandshell was built in 1929 at the instigation of prominent Stratford resident R. Thomas Orr who saw a similar building during his travels to California. It was the first bandshell built in Canada and was copied by others, most significantly by the Canadian National Exhibition in Toronto. The bandshell was located by the river so that the music could be heard throughout the city. The adjoining hill provided a natural amphitheatre.

LAKESIDE PARK, STRATFORD, ONT., CANADA.

Lakeside Park, circa 1920

Parks and Gardens

The parks system began to flourish in the early part of the century. In 1918, the first swans appeared on the river as part of an overall plan to improve the appearance of Lake Victoria and its shoreline. Almost from the beginning, the swans have been a symbol for Stratford and the parks system. R. Thomas Orr was the chief promoter of the parks system in Stratford for the first half of the twentieth century. Architect and insurance broker in his working life, he spent at least as much energy on his passions—literature, horticulture and heritage—which he pursued for the betterment of the city. His unflagging enthusiasm for each cause usually meant that he was put in charge and saw it through to the end.

His many projects can only be mentioned, but all of them had a significant impact on making Stratford what it is today. As member of the parks board (which he helped to create) from 1904 until his death in 1957, he pushed successfully for his dream of a park running the full length of the river. He led the campaign against a Canadian Pacific Railway line (which would have destroyed the park) for eight years until a referendum in 1912 voted in favour of the parks and against the CPR.

Another of Orr's projects was the Shakespearean Gardens, designed in 1936. Situated on the site of the Dufton Woollen Mills, the gardens were inspired and researched by Orr, who had visited Stratford-upon-Avon, England and decided Stratford, Canada needed a similar park. The park had samples of over sixty species of plants (many of which were brought back by Orr personally) mentioned in Shakespeare's plays. The gardens were opened during an official visit by Governor General Lord Tweedsmuir and his wife. Orr suggested that Queen Mary should donate roses to the gardens as she had done in England. She agreed, and they were sent to the gardens and planted in 1938.

A monument to Shakespeare was already suggested in 1922, but it was not until 1949 that sculptor

Cleve Horne of Toronto was commissioned by the Sons of England Lodge to create a bust to be placed in the gardens. Over the years there have been many renovations to the gardens and on July 18, 1980, they were re-dedicated by Lieutenant Governor Pauline McGibbon.

World War II

World War II deprived Stratford of many of its young and able-bodied men. It dramatically changed the social fabric of the community as women went to work in non-traditional jobs that took them away from the home and their families. Stratford's prominence as an industrial centre required labour, and it was women who provided it.

The normal production of the local furniture factories and CNR shops was interrupted as these workplaces switched to manufacturing for the war effort. Imperial Rattan Furniture Factory made spars for the Mosquito Bombers. Kroehler also contributed by making parts for Canadian war planes. Other locally made war materials included rubber parts for tanks and armoured cars and the brass parts and machine tools needed to make war equipment. Material for uniforms, gloves for the armed services and felt shoes were also made.

Various rallies and activities were held to raise money and collect recyclable products that could be used for the war effort. The local newspaper provided up-to-date coverage about the battles in Europe. It also reported on local soldiers and casualties. The newspaper was a vital source for encouraging people to remain positive and to do what they could at home. As soldiers returned, the paper reported on

their service records and made everyone feel that he or she was part of one big family sharing in the success of their local soldiers.

Many of the local men who served in World War II were in the Perth Regiment. The Perth Regiment had been a rifle battalion, but it was converted to machine guns in December, 1936. Being solidly prepared and organized, the regiment was mobilized on September 1, 1939, even before World War II began. However, despite continuous training, the regiment was not among the first sent overseas. In March, 1941, it was converted to a motor battalion within a tank brigade in the Fifth Armoured Division and finally sailed overseas in October, 1941.

In January, 1943, still in England, the regiment was converted again to an infantry battalion in the Eleventh Canadian Infantry Brigade. Finally, in October, 1943, the regiment was sent to the front in southern Italy, where fighting was heavy over the next year and a half. The regiment was transferred to the Netherlands in February, 1945. It fought with many other Canadians until the end of the war in Europe on May 5. The last man came home to Stratford on January 16, 1946.

Meanwhile, from January 1941 to the fall of 1942, Dutch citizens who lived in Canada, the United States and elsewhere responded to the call for help from their native country. They were stationed in the McLagan furniture factory on Trinity Street, which had been converted to barracks. Many contingents were trained here for active service. In some ways, these men took the place of the sons and husbands overseas. Stratford residents welcomed them into their homes and hoped that their men were being treated the same way. The result was strong friendships and even marriages.

A housewife or soldier's kit from World War II

Princess Juliana, later Queen of the Netherlands, who was living in Ottawa at the time, visited Stratford and the barracks sixteen times.

Following the war, the Dutch government presented Stratford with a monument featuring two hands holding an injured bird. The monument symbolized the relationship between Stratford and the Dutch troops and indicated the Netherlands' appreciation.

Postwar Period

When the war ended, industries returned to their regular trade and the war ration program was phased out. Many who returned from overseas had to be re-established in regular jobs and many more women remained in the workforce. The CNR shops were renovated and expanded in 1949. There seemed little reason to be worried, although the Industrial Commission, supported by the city and the chamber of commerce, continued to search for new businesses and industries.

Princess Juliana inspecting the Dutch troops, circa 1942

Stratford's prosperous existence had been shaken by the two world wars and the loss of its young men. The General Strike of 1933 had created a confrontational situation among city officials, industrial managers and the large working population. This animosity led to hard feelings for quite a few years, but World War II reunited Stratford residents, who worried about everyone sent to war.

Postwar Canada saw prosperity never before imagined. Canadians were introduced to modern technological advances like television, which soon began to replace the radio. People began to spend money and tried to forget the war and the Depression. Stratford residents believed that their lives were returning to normal. After all, thanks to the CNR shops and the furniture industry, Stratford continued to be a major industrial centre. This optimism would soon be tested

4

REVITALIZING STRATFORD

World War II introduced rapid advancements in technology that continued in the postwar era. These advancements had a major impact on the economy and on society, quickly making the old pre-war industries and lifestyles obsolete. This phenomenon caused a major transformation in Stratford as it did elsewhere. With the decline of many of its industries, Stratford was forced to re-invent itself as a modern industrial city. The change was successful because it was led from within by Stratford citizens rather than being imposed by outside forces. As a result, the city was able to control the growth and to build on what already existed.

Perth County Court House

Industrial Decline

In 1951, Canadian National Railways announced that because of the decline of the steam engine and the introduction of the diesel engine, the locomotive shops in Stratford would be gradually phased out. In 1958, came the further announcement that the shops would be closed as soon as possible. After more than seventy years, the residents and workers of Stratford could no longer rely on the railroad for employment. Of the 500 men still employed, 200 were laid off during that year. The CNR suggested that the remaining workers would be employed until they retired or another company purchased the buildings.

Stratford's other major industry, the furniture trade, had never recovered from the problems of the Depression. Many of the companies were gone. However, two firms—Kroehler and Imperial—had a renaissance in the 1950s and 1960s. Imperial pursued innovative modern furniture design and won a number of international awards during this period.

The shock of losing the CNR shops spurred the city council and the Industrial Commission to look actively for potential industries to settle in Stratford. The goal was to create a diversified industrial base with industries that had expansion potential. Creating a diversified base would eliminate the fear of a large employer downsizing that would reduce a significant part of the workforce to the ranks of the unemployed.

An Imperial Rattan rocker, circa 1930

The Industrial Commission, representing the city, the chamber of commerce and the Trades and Labour Council, prepared a profile of the community and a strategy to attract new industry. By approaching companies directly, attending trade shows and considering proposals from companies and individuals, the commission was successful in attracting over a dozen new manufacturers to the city by 1955.

New Industry

The campaign for new industry also led to the formation of the Stratford Shakespearean Festival in 1953. The resulting tourism industry has catapulted the city onto the world stage. Stratford quickly assumed two identities—manufacturing and theatre, a dichotomy that still exists very much today. Although the two groups have not always mixed easily, often seeming like two solitudes, their coexistence has contributed significantly to the continuing prosperity of the city.

Not all of the companies that settled in Stratford did so as part of a well-considered strategy. In 1953, Fischer AG of Germany had sent two representatives to look at a few prospective plant sites in Ontario. Because of personal connections, they had headed to the nearby town of Mitchell to take an unofficial look at a potential site there. Fortunately, they stopped in Stratford for coffee. The waitress overheard what they were talking about and, seeing the opportunity, called the chamber of commerce. Within minutes, Wilfrid Gregory, chairman of the Industrial Commission, appeared at the restaurant. After discussions over lunch, the company representatives returned to Toronto. Gregory had periodic contact with one of the representatives over the next few months until Fischer AG decided to negotiate for

Women workers in a Stratford factory, 1956

the plant has switched to specially made plastic parts for the automotive industry, although it still distributes the company's luggage products made elsewhere.

The largest manufacturing company today is Standard Products, an American company which came to Stratford after purchasing G. L. Griffith & Sons on Erie Street in 1966. The company's prosperity in making rubber parts for automobiles has led to the expansion of about nine plants in the city, employing about 1,300 people.

a site in Stratford. The original site shown them had already been taken in the meantime by FRAM, a manufacturer of automobile filters, so a new site farther east on Ontario Street was found. Today, FAG Bearings (formerly Fischer AG), which employs about 1,200 people, is one of the two largest companies in the city. It manufactures bearings for the automobile and aerospace industries and supplies companies all over the world.

New industry, largely from the automotive, metalworking and textile sectors, continued to arrive in Stratford in the 1960s through the efforts of the Industrial Commission. One widely known company was Samsonite, which arrived in 1955 to produce luggage. For many years, it also had the North American contract to make Lego. In recent years, production at

Although industry in the 1950s and 1960s was more diverse, today it has become concentrated in the automotive sector. All seven manufacturing companies with over 400 employees are automotive and the sector accounts for three-quarters (75 percent) of all manufacturing jobs and over a third (36 percent) of all jobs in the city. Manufacturing in all sectors accounts for about 50 percent of all jobs. Only two other companies, National Trust (which had its head office here) and the Stratford Festival, have more than 100 employees. Each has about 600.

The postwar growth and sense of optimism led to a demand for more houses. In every decade since the war, one or two major subdivisions have emerged, thereby extending the size of the city well past the older areas.

The first of these was a whole subdivision by the fairgrounds that was built immediately following World War II. These modern houses, better known as war-time or post-war houses, were inspired by American architect Frank Lloyd Wright's concept of suburbia. They were situated far enough from the downtown core to be a sanctuary for the people who lived in them. Mainly one and a half storey bungalows, they appealed to young families because of the modern facilities they offered.

Later subdivisions have followed the typical development trends of the period in which they were built and are similar to those elsewhere in Ontario. These include Avonwood, Queensland, Mornington Heights, Avon Heights and Greenwood.

Growth brought about the need for a new hospital. By 1948, plans for one had been approved and the Stratford General Hospital was completed in 1950. Over the years, there have been many renovations and additions. Most recently, the front lobby was expanded and CAT scan facilities were provided. A palliative care ward was also added. The old hospital, known as Avoncrest, now holds hospital administration.

Bungalows, like the ones shown here, were popular after World War II

Stratford's city hall, slated for demolition in 1969, was saved by concerned citizens

completion of the new federal building on Waterloo Street. This began a trend in demolishing the old to build the new. In 1964, a suggestion by Mayor C. H. Meier that city hall should be demolished for a new development that would accommodate a hotel for tourists as well as city hall offices began an argument that took several years to resolve. In 1969, when the council agreed to demolish the late Victorian landmark, six women in Stratford spearheaded the "Save the City Hall League" and approached the council with a petition to retain the building. This issue was not resolved until 1972, when the developer finally withdrew from the discussion and the city hall was spared.

With the creation of the Shakespearean Festival, tourism became a very important source of revenue for the city. Although they come to see the plays, visitors also enjoy the parks and the Victorian character of the downtown and the older neighbourhoods. These were the features that created a beautiful setting for the festival in the first place. This history would not be complete without referring to the movements that emerged to keep prominent landmarks from destruction during the postwar era of "progress."

Preserving Stratford's Heritage

In the early 1960s, the post office building and the Perth Mutual building were demolished following

The "Save the City Hall League" regrouped as the "Citizens for Stratford" movement to ensure that other civic matters were addressed in accordance with the citizens' views. In 1974, another battle was soon to follow when the Gordon and Idington Blocks, two prominent Victorian buildings on Downie Street, were slated for demolition to make room for the ARCOM project, a hotel complex. Heritage Stratford was formed by some of the veterans of the city hall battle to oppose the re-development. Eventually, a developer from London with a heritage interest was able to buy the Gordon and Idington blocks and renovate them as the Festival Square. The Ontario Heritage Foundation has an easement on the building to ensure heritage standards are maintained.

Meanwhile, in 1977 the Royal Bank, housed in an excellent example of Victorian architecture located on a prominent corner downtown, decided it wanted to modernize and rebuild. Heritage Canada member Pierre Berton wrote a letter to the mayor of Stratford denouncing the city's decision to let the Royal Bank demolish its structure. In the middle of this public outcry, the building was destroyed. Shortly afterward the building housing the Toronto-Dominion Bank and the Bank of Commerce were also destroyed. New,

modern buildings replaced these structures on the corners across from city hall.

Eventually, guidelines were developed for referring building changes to the Local Architectural Conservation Advisory Committee, as the city has become more aware of the heritage value of the downtown.

As early as 1989, this committee and the City Centre Committee were encouraging a heritage designation of the downtown core in order to conserve, protect and promote what was already there. In April, 1998, an Ontario Municipal Board adjudicator heard the reasons for and against such a designation. Within a month a decision had been given. The downtown

Festival Square, spared demolition, was renovated as a heritage site in 1974

The Brandenburger Block was built in 1873.

parks system and some of the older treed areas. The T. J. Dolan nature trail was established as a tribute to Dolan, a longtime member of the parks board. Maintenance projects to prevent erosion of the Avon river banks were also done in several phases. The parks board created an arboretum on the south side of Delamere Avenue near the Victorian Inn with labels identifying the trees. Meadowrue Gardens began featuring flora and fauna native to this area. A celebration of the swans takes place in March every year when a parade, accompanied by local dignitaries and pipers, marches from the swans' home to the Avon River.

would have a heritage designation. The adjudicator ruled in favour of the designation, partly because of the tourism that Stratford attracts.

Together with the County of Perth, the city established an archives in 1972 to preserve the important records of the municipal governments and to record the history of the whole county through documents, photographs, maps and so on. The Stratford-Perth Archives celebrated its twenty-fifth anniversary in 1997 and is the second-oldest county archives in Ontario. Efforts to found a museum for the display of artefacts of local significance continued for many years until 1993, when the first display was opened. The Gallery Stratford, originally sponsored by Rothman's, was established in 1967 in the historic old pump house on Romeo Street and across the park from the Festival Theatre.

Just as a heritage movement developed to save significant buildings, an environmental movement began with the objective of preserving the Avon River, the

But civic pride perhaps reached its height when Stratford won the 1997 title of most beautiful city in the world for the Nations in Bloom contest. The international Nations in Bloom Competition is a non-profit initiative of the International Federation of Parks and Recreation Administration. Corporate sponsors from all over the world support this competition where communities are judged in categories dependent on their population. Judging criteria include heritage preservation, environmentally sensitive practices, enhancement of landscape and community involvement.

Today, Stratford continues on the course it set in the 1950s. Its focus is on growth in moderate-sized industrial plants and in the continued development of the attractiveness of the city for visitors and residents alike. This strategy is one that is in step with the prevailing belief in a controlled growth that will not disrupt the appeal of the community.

The Avon River

5

THE STRATFORD FESTIVAL

"With one bold stroke that has left our big cities gasping, Stratford, Ont., will this summer claim its birthright with a Shakespearean festival." This was how *Maclean's* magazine saw the beginning of the Stratford Shakespearean Festival in 1953. It was bold indeed for an upstart community of 19,000 to think of establishing a permanent professional theatre in a country that had only half a dozen professional theatre companies and various summer stock companies. Yet the Stratford Festival has succeeded in becoming the largest classical repertory theatre in North America.

The Festival Theatre

The Origins

The Canada Company had created the birthright by naming the town after Shakespeare's home, and various leading citizens over the years had taken the Shakespearean connection seriously. Perhaps it was natural then for Tom Patterson, a student at Stratford's collegiate in the 1930s, to dream of a Shakespearean festival while pondering the future of the city with his school chums in the Shakespearean Gardens next to the school.

What made the idea a reality was the coincidence of a number of events in 1951. It was in this year that the

Hunter publication. Patterson wrote on various aspects of public works. Early in 1951, at a Waterworks conference in Winnipeg, he ran into Stratford's mayor, David Simpson and raised the idea of a Shakespearean festival as he had done with other Stratford residents and politicians before. The mayor's surprisingly upbeat response sparked Patterson to actively pursue the formation of the festival.

After talking to various people in government and arts circles, he built up the confidence to approach the city council. In January, 1952, he presented his idea and requested $100 to go to New York to meet Sir Laurence Olivier. The council gave him $125.

Tom Patterson's short presentation to council seemed to catch the imagination of the local newspaper as a natural idea for the city. On January 22, 1952, the headline of the Stratford Beacon Herald read: "COUNCIL TOLD OF IDEA TO MAKE STRATFORD WORLD FAMOUS SHAKE-SPEAREAN CENTRE". The article began confidently: "Dreams of Stratford as an even greater cultural centre..." The article reflected the community's sense that somehow it was already more "cultural" than other places in the area. Soon the piece was being repeated in newspapers all across the country.

In New York, Patterson never did meet Sir Laurence Olivier, but he did visit the Carnegie and Rockefeller foundations. Although he received nothing but best wishes, he felt encouraged and continued exploring the idea. An already existing committee of the chamber of commerce studying a suggestion to have minstrels in the park during the summer, also became charged with the festival project. Soon all other ideas were dropped and Tom Patterson's idea became the focus of the committee.

Through fortunate meetings in Toronto with CBC producer Mavor Moore and his mother Dora Mavor

Tyrone Guthrie and Tom Patterson, 1953

city council and the chamber of commerce began seriously looking for new industries to settle in Stratford. The announcement that the CNR shops would be phased out, together with the serious decline in the furniture industry, were warning signs that this initiative had some urgency. But the desire to revitalize Stratford also had much to do with the beginning of a new decade which looked forward to developing new ideas after the years of war and reconstruction. Among those people who came forward with proposals to the chamber and the city council was Tom Patterson.

After returning from the war overseas, Patterson had attended Trinity College in Toronto and then obtained a position on *Civic Administration*, a Maclean

Moore, director of The New Play Society, Tom Patterson received his first firm commitment. Dora Mavor Moore suggested that Patterson contact the great Shakespearean director, Tyrone Guthrie, with whom she was well acquainted. This fitted Patterson's own inclination perfectly—start with the best. And so,

From left to right: Dr. Harrison Showalter, Judy Guthrie, Tyrone Guthrie, and Tanya Moiseiwitsch at the Stratford train station, 1953

after preliminary correspondence between Moore and Guthrie, Patterson proceeded to call Guthrie at his home in rural Ireland. Thinking the call from Toronto a crank, the operator simply hung up the first time, but eventually Patterson got through. After an exchange of letters and another phone call, Guthrie arrived in Stratford in July, 1952.

Tom Patterson

Guthrie writes that he expected to find a typical committee consisting "mainly of artistic and excitable elderly ladies of both sexes, with a sprinkling of Business Men to restrain the Artistic People from spending money..." Instead, to his surprise, "most of the members of the committee were quite young. I was almost the oldest person present...the males outnumbered the females by about five to one."

What appealed to Guthrie was that Patterson and the committee admitted that they knew nothing about theatre or its operation and had no existing facility in which to produce it. The open-air bandshell had been ruled out at once. They were giving Guthrie a free hand to develop all the aspects of the theatre.

For years, Guthrie had been a proponent of performing Shakespearean plays on the type of stage Shakespeare would have used. Here was the opportunity to build just such a revolutionary thrust stage. It

Cecil Clarke and Tanya Moiseiwitsch with a set model, 1953

and summer stock companies that operated with difficulty in Canada and in the CBC radio drama program.

For the first season, which opened July 13, 1953, Guthrie chose two contrasting plays *Richard III* and *All's Well that Ends Well*. Guthrie and Moiseiwitsch proceeded with designing the thrust stage and overseeing its construction. In contrast to the typical proscenium stage which is removed from the audience, the thrust stage is surrounded by the audience on three sides and allows the performance to be more intimate and inter-active. Local contractor Gaffney began building the amphitheatre.

The board of directors of the new Stratford Festival Foundation, formed in November, 1952, with Dr. Harry Showalter as president and Tom Patterson as general manager, had a very large task in raising enough money to meet building costs. Up until the very last minute, there were times when the whole project was almost cancelled, but finally

was soon decided that this stage would be built within a concrete amphitheatre, the whole covered by a spe-cially made tent. (A permanent building was thought premature until the festival had proven itself.)

In the area of production, Guthrie insisted on star performers and experienced theatre personnel (actors, designers, artisans and so on). The commit-tee's firm commitment to his ideas and terms intrigued Guthrie, and he accepted the position of director for the first season.

Longtime associates of Guthrie, production manag-er Cecil Clarke and designer Tanya Moiseiwitsch, were brought from Britain as well as the heads of the wardrobe and properties departments. The star attrac-tion was popular British film and stage actor Alec Guinness, who turned down a number of more secure offers including one from the Royal Shakespeare Company in England. Except for three other actors, including Irene Worth, who were brought from Britain, the rest of the cast and crew were Canadians, many of them trained in the few professional theatre

Robert Goodier as Richmond and Alec Guiness as King Richard in Richard III, *directed by Tyrone Guthrie and designed by Tanya Moiseiwitsch, 1953*

some large donations came through which helped to meet the immediate bills, especially the tent being made in Chicago, which was on hold pending a further installment. Fortunately, the local contractor continued to build even when he was not sure that he would ever be paid.

Credit is due to those Stratford citizens who stuck with the project through its highs and lows. In the end, the first season was so successful that it was extended from five to six weeks and had a deficit of only $4,000 despite exceeding by $60,000 the original budget of $150,000. (The festival raised $157,000 in donations; the rest was ticket sales.) Every performance was sold out and some were oversold, requiring extra chairs to be placed in the aisles and along the edge of the stage.

As *Maclean's* foresaw, "with one bold stroke" Guthrie's creation at Stratford set new professional standards that had a profound impact on theatre in Canada and probably in North America. Canadian writer Merill Denison later summed it up: "It never could have happened anywhere else."

Festival Actors and Staff

Since the first season of the festival, the actors have been accepted by the residents of Stratford as part of the community. A first-season garden party was held inviting the residents to see the location of the theatre, which was virtually a hole in the ground, and to meet the actors. Many of the actors were invited to dinner at various homes. As compensation for their meals, the actors would provide entertainment and everyone would feel they had benefitted from the evening. Usually it was politicians or the arts supporters who invited the actors, allowing them the prestige of saying who had come to dinner. Sundays provided another chance for social mingling as there were no performances. Many of the actors would go to the quarries in St. Marys, a popular swimming place, to relax.

During the early years, few members of the acting company resided in Stratford year-round. Today many actors live in town or in the surrounding area all year long, which allows them to be close to the festival and within a commutable distance to Toronto. Stratford also offers affordable housing and for those raising a family, its community life and atmosphere are ideal. Some of the actors that make their

Children raising money for the festival, 1953

home in Stratford include Martha Henry, Douglas Rain, Mervyn Blake, William Needles, William Hutt, Richard Monette, Goldie Semple, Lorne Kennedy, Keith Dinicol and Colm Feore. Following performances, actors who are unwinding often meet in the local pubs. Residents of Stratford respect the privacy of the actors and their families.

Many of the people who work behind the scenes also live here year-round, including designers Polly Bodhanetsky and Susan Benson. The festival employs between 600 and 800 people during the year. Stratford residents work in the festival's administration, production and props, costumes and other technical departments. During the summer, students serve as ushers and box office assistants. In the off-season, the festival's props department and other artists contract their services to other theatres. Props and costumes for Toronto's popular *Cats* musical, for example, were done by the artists at the festival.

The Stratford Festival has today acquired the importance that the CNR shops once had. It touches the lives of a very large number of families in Stratford. And yet, some residents have still never been to a festival production nor have the desire to do so.

The Festival Company and staff are valuable members of the community. Many support the fundraising efforts of local groups as well as provide input to changes that could affect Stratford.

Rehearsal, 1953. Back row: Elspeth Potter, John Hayes. Centre row, from left to right: Richard Easton, Peter Mews, Timothy Findley, Bill Needles, Eric House, Bill Hutt, Roland Bull, Robert Christie, Douglas Rain, Robert Robinson, Alex Smith, Betty Leighton, Norman Roland. Front row, from left to right: Irene Worth, Robert Goodier, Bruce Swerdfager, Amelia Hall

Stratford's Theatres

Almost as important to the success of the festival as the performances themselves and the name and parklike setting of the city is the Festival Theatre building. The theatre's unusual design has become a key asset in the promotion of the festival and Stratford. The novelty of the original tent used during the first four seasons was preserved in the design and distinctive roofline of the Festival Theatre building erected in 1957.

The amphitheatre, designed by architect Robert Fairfield of Toronto, and the thrust stage of the theatre were built in 1953 in preparation for the first season. The whole was covered with a tent measuring 150 feet

Dr. H.A. Showalter turns the sod for the festival tent, 1953

The tent going up over the stage, 1953

in diameter and 61 feet from stage to peak. The stage sat directly below the peak in the very centre of the theatre. The canvas weighed over 3 tons and was tied down with 10 miles of rope and 2 miles of cable. The amphitheatre also had a diameter of 150 feet and was dug 24 feet into the ground. Seating capacity was about 1,500. At the end of each season the tent was taken down to be put up again the following spring. During the first four seasons under the tent 400,000 visitors saw 260 stage performances, occasionally accompanied by thunderstorms and train whistles.

At the end of the 1956 season the tent came down immediately so that work on a new permanent building could begin. The tent was cut up into small pieces, which were pasted on specially printed cards and sold to the public as mementos.

The new building, also designed by architect Robert Fairfield, was circular, 200 feet in diameter and about 70 feet high with the peak again immediately above the stage. The extra diameter was included for a lobby and workspace. With a balcony above the amphitheatre, seating was increased to 2,276. Through the Herculean efforts of Gaffney Construction of Stratford and some 150 workers, the building was finished in time for its dedication on June 30, 1957 and the opening of the fifth season the next day. In 1958, Fairfield won the Massey Gold Medal for Architecture for his innovative design of the building.

A major addition to the backstage area was completed in 1985 as part of the festival's "Next Stage" building campaign. The architects were the Barton Myers Associates of Toronto in consultation with Robert Fairfield. The enlarged facilities have allowed all properties and costumes to be made on the premises. As well as administrative offices, dressing rooms and staff cafeteria, the backstage area contains the wardrobe workshops, the properties workshops, the wig room, a laundry room and a rehearsal hall. Above and behind the stage is the orchestra loft.

In 1997, the "Act III" building campaign was completed. It saw major renovations to the auditorium and additions to the front and rear of the building. The old amphitheatre was completely replaced by a new one with wider and higher tiers and the arc of the auditorium was reduced eliminat-

Visitors tour the warehouse

ing the two outer aisles which did not have a clear view of the stage. This reduced the number of seats by 450, but those that remain are now more comfortable. As part of this renovation, a new tunnel was also constructed in the "underworld" to make it easier for actors to get from one side of the stage to the other.

The lobby areas were expanded by an addition to the front of the building. The theatre store has been placed between the two lobbies and additional space has been created for the box office, an elevator and washrooms. A new marquee was added to the side of the building facing the river as well. The architect was Thomas Payne of Kuwabara Payne McKenna Blumberg in consultation with festival designers Tanya Moiseiwitsch and Desmond Heeley.

The key feature of the Festival Theatre is the thrust stage that Tanya Moiseiwitsch designed for the first season in 1953. It originally had nine posts under the balcony with side doors entering the landings halfway down the balcony stairs on each side. The stairs descended to points under the balcony. Slight alterations were made to the stage when the Festival Theatre was built in 1957, but the major revision was made in 1962 in what director Michael Langham termed a "change of sex." Langham considered the stage too "feminine." The number of posts were reduced to five and the side doors and stairs were moved outward.

Other slight changes to the stage were made in 1975, but these were all reversed by 1981. The balcony, however, no longer rests on its pillars and can be used without them or removed altogether.

As the festival expanded its program to include

The Avon Theatre

music and film festivals and later more theatre productions, it became necessary to find new performance spaces in Stratford. Starting in 1956, the festival rented the Avon Theatre on Downie Street. The Avon was originally opened in 1901 as a vaudeville house known as the Theatre Albert. It became the Majestic movie theatre in the 1930s and was renamed the Avon about 1942.

The building was purchased by the festival in 1963 at which time the interior was remodelled to include enlarged stage facilities and an auditorium seating about 1,100. The exterior was redesigned by architects John B. Parkin Associates in 1967. Further interior changes were made in 1975, 1981 and 1986, and as part of the "Next Stage" building campaign in 1985, a three-storey building was added on the back. The scenery-production workshop and the festival's membership office are located here, as well as extra dressing rooms, rehearsal halls and offices. The Avon provides a traditional proscenium stage which has been used for Gilbert and Sullivan musicals, Mozart operas and more modern plays, as well as some Shakespeare.

The need for a more flexible theatre for contemporary or experimental productions and for workshops led to the opening in 1971 of the Third Stage in the casino belonging to the Stratford Badminton Club on Lakeside Drive. Public performances have been produced here almost every year since then. It has been the home of the Young Company since its founding in 1975, although members now appear in all of the festival's regular productions. In 1991, the facility was renamed the Tom Patterson Theatre, in honour of the festival's founder. After a number of changes over the years, it now seats 500.

Drama, Music, Film and Art

The mainstay of the Stratford Festival has been the thirty-seven plays of Shakespeare. Some favourites have been performed in eight of the festival's forty-eight seasons (*As You Like It*, *A Midsummer Night's Dream*, *Much Ado About Nothing* and *Twelfth Night*), others in seven (*King Lear*, *Love's Labour Lost*, *Macbeth*, *Romeo and Juliet* and *The Taming of the Shrew*) while less-popular plays have been performed in at least two seasons (*Cymbeline*, *King Henry IV Part 2*, *King Henry VI*, *King Henry VIII*, *Timon of Athens*, and *Troilus and Cressida*).

However, many other plays in the classical reper-

The Tom Patterson Theatre

toire, as well as some by contemporary Canadian playwrights, have been produced as well. Some of these have been performed in as many as four seasons (*The Importance of Being Earnest, Oedipus Rex, Tartuffe* and *Waiting for Godot*) or three seasons (*Cyrano de Bergerac, The Cherry Orchard, The Country Wife, Long Day's Journey into Night* and *She Stoops to Conquer*). *Alice Through the Looking Glass* by Stratford-born Canadian playwright James Reaney has been produced in two seasons (1994, 1996).

The productions and operation of the festival have been the responsibility of the artistic directors: Tyrone Guthrie (1953, 1955), Cecil Clarke (1954), Michael Langham (1956–67), Jean Gascon (1968–74), Robin Phillips (1975–80), John Hirsch (1981–85), John Neville (1986–89), David William (1990–93) and

Richard Monette (1994–). They have worked with a board of governors that in the early years was drawn largely from Stratford but is now chosen from a wider geographical area.

Musical theatre and opera have also been performed regularly over the years. Gilbert and Sullivan operettas have been the most popular, especially *The Mikado, The Gondoliers, H. M. S. Pinafore* and *The Pirates of Penzance*. Music concerts were also held starting in 1953. They evolved into an organized music festival from 1955 through 1975 that was performed in various locations throughout the city. Some of the artists featured were Glenn Gould, Claudio Arrau, Isaac Stern, Itzhak Perlman, Leonard Rose, Rudolf Serkin, Jean-Pierre Rampal, Julian Bream, Alexandre Lagoya, Ravi Shankar, Oscar Peterson, Duke

The Two Gentlemen of Verona, *1998. From left to right: Rory Feore as the Court Painter, Wayne Best as Turio, John Dolan as Eglamour, Tamara Bernier as Silvia, John Gilbert as the Duke of Milan, and Graham Abbey as Valentine*

The Mikado, 1993. From left to right: Thomas Goerz as Pish-Tush, Doug MacNaughton as a Gentleman of Japan, Timothy French as a Gentleman of Japan, John Avey as the Mikado of Japan, Christina James as Katisha, John Watson as a Gentleman of Japan, and Jim White as a Gentleman of Japan

artistic director Elyakim Taussig and a local board of directors was created. It operated for four seasons from 1981 through 1984, with most concerts held in the city hall auditorium. It featured various artists, including Liona Boyd, the Canadian Brass, Moe Koffman, Rob McConnell, Camerata, Moshe Hammer and Salome Bey. Although Summer Music folded in 1984, one lasting outcome was the Stratford Concert Choir.

The music directors of the Stratford Festival have been Louis Applebaum (1953–60), Glenn Gould/Leonard Rose/Oscar Shumsky (1961–64), Oscar Shumsky (1965–67), Victor de Bello (1968–69), André Gingras (1970–73), Raffi Armenian (1973–76) and Berthold Carrière (1976–present). Besides musical productions and concert programs, they have also composed incidental music for some of the plays.

Ellington, Dave Brubeck, Phil Nimmons, Ed McCurdy, Lois Marshall, Maureen Forrester, Jon Vickers, Louis Quillico and the Hungarian Quartet, the Oxford Quartet and the Vaghy Quartet.

The final years under music director Raffi Armenian, also music director of the Kitchener-Waterloo Symphony Orchestra (KWSO), saw the creation of the Stratford Festival Ensemble (later renamed the Canadian Chamber Ensemble) which has become one of the leading chamber groups in Canada as well as the core of the KWSO.

After the music festival had been discontinued, attempts were made to create an organization separate from the festival to revive it. In 1980, Stratford Summer Music under

Festival directors, 1960. From left to right: Victor Di Bello, Leonard Rose, Oscar Shumsky, and Louis Applebaum

An International Film Festival, accompanied by lectures, symposia and retrospectives, was held from

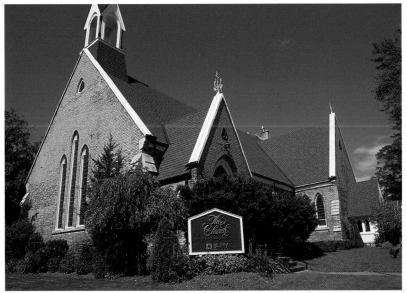

The Church Restaurant

1956 through 1961 and again from 1971 through 1975 featuring contemporary films from over forty countries. Many of the films had their Canadian, North American or sometimes even world premiere at this festival. Like the music festival, the film festival was discontinued after the 1975 season as the focus shifted to theatre alone under artistic director Robin Phillips.

Since its beginning, the festival has also sponsored art and theatre exhibitions in Stratford. After 1969, this was often done in conjunction with The Gallery Stratford. It has also prepared exhibitions that have toured Canada and the U. S. and lent items to exhibitions around the world.

The festival has produced full-length feature films of various plays over the years, as well as audio recordings, television productions, radio broadcasts and two series of texts. Many documentaries have also been produced, among them The Stratford Adventure, produced in 1954 by the National Film Board about the founding of the festival. Many books have been written about the festival's seasons and productions. The records of the festival, along with some representative costumes and props, have been preserved in the Stratford Festival Archives founded in 1967. The active collection of costumes and props from past productions (available for reuse or rental) is stored in the costume warehouse which is open for public tours twice a week.

The festival also has an ongoing education program of student matinees, school lectures, teaching aids and annual teacher seminars. This program has inspired many English and drama teachers across Ontario and in the nearby U. S. to study a Shakespeare play in class before making the annual trip to the festival. About 60,000 students attend performances every year.

The Festival and Tourism

Tourism has become an important industry in Stratford with the economic benefit for the community at about $125,000,000 in 1998. This includes accommodation, dining, shopping and other expenses incurred by tourists. Over the years this amount has grown and the city has grown to meet the needs of visitors.

When the festival first opened, a train sponsored by the *Toronto Telegram* took patrons to Stratford's train station where they boarded a bus to either Parkview United Church or Knox Presbyterian Church for a lunch provided by the women's groups. Following this, they were taken to the theatre and then returned to

York Street

their businesses through the winter months. This is especially true in some of the specialty shops and boutiques that have appeared. Today, dining options range from chain restaurants to four-star cuisine offered at the Church, Rundles and the Old Prune. A chef's school was even started to train budding chefs who would then be employed in Stratford's restaurants. Local chefs and artists teach students different facets of food preparation and design. City residents are invited to sample the students' meals at reduced prices, thus allowing the students a chance to practise and the residents a chance to enjoy excellent cuisine.

One of the most obvious effects of tourism on the community, apart from the economic one, is the Friends of the Festival support group. This group of about 150 people are volunteers who work with the staff of the festival to promote and enhance the projects that are underway. They provide volunteer time in the store, at information desks, at the warehouse, archives, library and even some of the fundraising events. In 1996, the Friends of the Festival members were nominated by the Stratford Shakespearean Festival Foundation for an Outstanding Achievement Award sponsored by the provincial government. This award was presented to them at a ceremony in London by representatives of the Ministry of Citizenship, Culture and Recreation. Many of the people who belong to this group are bed and breakfast owners, local business people or people who believe in the festival and the importance of what it contributes to theatre and to the City of Stratford.

Over the years, the Shakespearean festival has become a crucial element in Stratford's economy as well as a cultural treasure for the entire country. The festival's success has made Stratford a world-famous tourist destination and has also helped shape the city's unique and vibrant identity.

the train for the trip home. There were very few restaurants at the time and even fewer hotels. Tourists were billeted with residents or they could stay at the local YMCA.

In 1951, there were 18 restaurants, 1 motel and 7 hotels. By 1998, the numbers had increased to 78 restaurants, 11 motels, 6 hotels and 1 guest house. There are also over 250 bed and breakfast facilities in Stratford. This includes the special guesthouses that are booked exclusively through the Festival Theatre.

Downtown merchants rely on tourist dollars to help

STRATFORD'S HERITAGE: A WALKING TOUR

Stratford's charm and picturesque setting make it the perfect location for a Shakespearean festival, while its architecture attracts people interested in the history of the area. This walking tour will highlight some of the important historic sites in the community as well as introduce you to its rich architectural heritage.

The Canada Company had planned Stratford to develop north of the river. However, the railroad's arrival in 1857 enticed people south. This tour will focus on the downtown and the old residential neighbourhood north of the river that was built before the railroad's influence.

Market Place (1)

Market Place was originally owned by surveyor  Donald McDonald who sold the property to the Town of Stratford in the 1850s with the condition that it would always be used as a gathering place for people and not for a municipal building. Nevertheless, the first town hall was built here in 1857. It was a large neoclassical building, far grander than Stratford's population required. To meet McDonald's condition, a market was held where the present parking lot stands. The town hall had stalls that faced it.

City Hall (2)

The queen of the square was built between 1898–1899. It replaced the earlier town hall which was destroyed by fire in 1897. Toronto architect George W. King designed the building, which fit into a triangular site. The idea was that there would be no back entrance.

Built in true Victorian style, complete with contrasting materials, textures, many windows and the

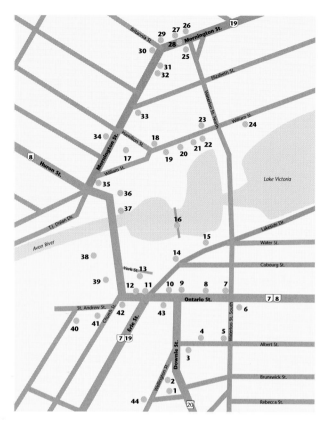

Now the home of Canada Trust, the only part of the original block is 23 Albert Place. For many years, the Windsor Block was an important anchor and landmark in the downtown core. It was built in 1871 as a hotel.

Cross to the north side of the block and go east past the parking lot to 42 Albert Street.

borrowing of architectural features from other styles, this building was threatened with demolition during the 1960s. Luckily, it was saved and has since been revitalized with several renovations. On July 1, 1998, Lieutenant Governor Hilary Weston joined the community in re-dedicating the building for the next hundred years with a time capsule.

Cross the street to the Canada Trust building.

Windsor Block (3)
Although it was common for buildings to be named after their owners, this building digressed from the norm and was called the Windsor Block, in keeping with Stratford's British connection. Initially the block extended to Downie Street, but over the years it has been replaced with different commercial buildings.

Albert Street (4)
Professional offices are now housed at 42 Albert Street. This building was constructed in 1888 by Catherine Beutter and operated as a boardinghouse. The railroad's prosperity in the 1850s meant that buildings like this were needed for railroad workers or for weary visitors waiting for a train connection.

Continue to Waterloo Street and turn north.

The Armoury, 80 Waterloo Street (5)

The Armoury is a federal building constructed in

1905 in a baronial style that was common at the end of the Victorian period. It remains an important landmark in the city and operates today as a militia training centre.

Queen's Inn, 161 Ontario Street (6)

This neoclassical building was constructed around 1906 by owner Fred Corrie. It replaced the original

wooden hotel built in 1855, which was destroyed by a fire. This building has been designated under the Ontario Heritage Act as a significant heritage property. It was restored during the 1980s by the owners of the Elora Old Mill restaurant and continues to be well maintained.

Knox Presbyterian Church, 142 Ontario Street (7)

Try to imagine a steeple that is 227 feet high and can be seen for miles. The previous Knox Church had

such a steeple. Its height set a standard for other buildings on Ontario Street to emulate. The courthouse was built to match as was the Gordon Block (10 Downie Street) and numbers 70–76 Ontario Street. Stratford was devastated when this church was struck by lightning in 1913 and three people were killed in the ensuing fire, including the fire chief.

The church was rebuilt in 1913 in the Gothic revival style, which allowed rounder details than the earlier pointed Gothic style. It has been designated a heritage building. All that remains of the original church is located at the back on Waterloo Street.

Continue west on Ontario Street.

Ontario Street (8)

Stratford's Victorian charm is noticeable on both sides of these two blocks. Originally, commercial buildings were frame. As merchants became more prosperous with Stratford's commercial growth, brick buildings were constructed.

Buildings were twinned or matched for consistency, with a second storey added, followed by a third storey at a later date. The third storey identifies these buildings as Victorian. Note the decorative cornice, finials and other details near the soffits. Much of this tinwork was produced by artisans at the Grand Trunk Railway (CNR) shops. Note as well that care has been taken to give the streetscape continuity—even the windows are level. Plaques mark the buildings at Bentley's and Gordon's Men Wear.

Continue east to the traffic lights and cross to the north side of Ontario Street.

Shakespeare Inn Monument (9)

Thomas Mercer Jones named Stratford after giving local innkeeper William Sargint a portrait of William Shakespeare. This was the earliest hotel in Stratford, erected by the Canada Company to service settlers in the area. The Shakespeare Inn was located here until it was destroyed by fire in 1849. This marker commemorates the building as a significant site in Stratford's history.

Surveying Site (10)

This site is almost immediately adjacent to the Shakespeare Inn. It was here that the early surveyors began measuring to create the town plan. The main streets Erie, Ontario and Huron, meet at this point and are named after the lakes that they head toward.

Continue west and cross the street.

Wade's Flowers, 54 Ontario Street (11)

Wade's Flowers was the location of Peter Wood's Albion Hotel. Built in the early 1850s, this building was where churches congregated, municipal meetings were held and people went to relax. In 1863, a riot broke out during a premature celebration for political candidate Thomas Mayne Daly. Daly's supporters found out that he had in fact lost to opponent Robert McFarlane. When McFarlane's supporters paraded past the building, Daly's men began to throw stones and attack the parade. This was also the location where Thomas Edison stayed in 1863.

Mill Block, 2–54 Ontario Street (12)

The Mill Block is the oldest commercial business block in Stratford. Built during the 1850s and early

1860s, it features some interesting Victorian details and the merchants continue to maintain and restore what is there. Built on a natural cliff, the back of this block has an additional lower storey. Many of these lower storeys were used as storage or unloading space for the businesses on Ontario Street. This changed during the 1980s.

Walk north past Wade's to York Street.

York Street (13)

In the 1980s, York Street became a popular commercial area featuring many attractive boutiques and shops. Take some time now to browse or return to this area at the end of your tour.

Cross the street and continue on to the War Memorial.

War Memorial, Lakeside Drive (14)

Following World War I, veterans of the Great War wanted to construct a monument to commemorate their comrades who had died. It was not until the 1920s that the Independent Order of the Daughters

of the Empire supported the push for a monument and began working with members of the Great War Veterans' Association to fulfil their wish. Their efforts were successful and in 1922 Canadian sculptor Walter Allward was commissioned with the classical theme of right versus might. These bronze statues show the victorious right defeating the defiant might. Originally placed at the corner of Erie and Ontario Streets, the monument was moved here during the 1960s. Allward is famous for the National War Memorial in Ottawa and the memorial at Vimy Ridge.

Follow Lakeside Drive east to the bandshell.

The Bandshell, Lakeside Drive (15)

Every community used to have an octagonal bandstand that was used in celebrations. In 1939, R. Thomas Orr proposed the bandshell design, based on one he saw during a trip to California. It was approved and was the first to be built in Ontario. The bandshell at the Canadian National Exhibition was based on this design, as was the bandshell in London. It was designated as a heritage building and is still used today for outdoor concerts.

Retrace your steps to the tourist information booth. Proceed to the dam walkway and turn north.

R.T. Orr Dam (16)

Without this dam, the Avon River would revert to being a small creek about four feet wide and one foot deep. This is the seventh dam to be located here. Named after one of the fathers of Stratford, R. Thomas Orr, it is a prominent site used as a walkway between the commercial area and the residential area north of the river.

Continue north to William Street. Cross the road to St. James Anglican Church.

St. James Anglican Church, 41 Mornington Street (17)

St. James Anglican Church was built in the Gothic tradition, with the emphasis on pointed features. It

was constructed by local contractor John Holmes between 1868 and 1870. The graveyard is the last one in Stratford that is attached to a church. Many of the old tombstones have fallen over, but can still be seen. The interior of the church has blue carpet from Queen

Elizabeth II's coronation. Many of the iron details were made by local artisans at the GTR shops.

Cross Hamilton Street and continue south to William Street.

Old Courthouse, William Street at Hamilton Street (18)

Stratford's first courthouse was located at the corner of William and Hamilton Streets overlooking the river. Its prominent location north of the river attests to the Canada Company's initial plan to have Stratford develop north. It was built in 1853 by local architect Peter Ferguson. Within a few years, it became obvious that the building was too small and the smell from the jail, immediately behind on Elizabeth Street, prevented the magistrates from holding court sessions. The building was eventually demolished when the new courthouse was built. Around 1900 a number of houses were constructed on the site.

69 William Street (19)

Across the street is one of the early residences of Stratford, 69 William.

This two story Georgian revival style building, complete with neoclassical quoins, was built during the late 1850s. The sympathetic addition was added later.

Continue east to 101 and 109 William Street.

The Twins, 101 and 109 William Street (20 and 21)

Before William Street was residential, planing mills were located on both sides of the river. One of the most important mill barons of the time was William Easson. The houses at 101 and 109 William Street were built in 1908 for two of his children. Known in the family as the "twins," these two houses were constructed identically to avoid any protests of favouritism. These excellent examples of Italianate homes have since been slightly altered on the outside.

Avon Castle, 113 William Street (22)

Easson's prosperity is obvious when looking at his residence at 113 William Street which was built in the early 1850s. Avon Castle was originally a smaller regency cottage with a second and third storey added

in 1867. The house is in the Second Empire style complete with a mansard roof and decorative brackets. The addition of the mansard roof shows how a new style building is created when changes are made to the original.

Continue to 140 William Street.

Copybook house, 140 William Street (23)

Copybook houses like 140 William Street were popular when the later Italianate homes and Queen Anne revival styles were being built. House designs were featured in trade magazines and books, allowing contractors to build similar homes with reversed floor plans. This house was built in 1903.

Cross the street and walk on the south side of William Street to number 203.

MacLennan House, 203 William Street (24)

Sir John Cunningham MacLennan was an important scientist who discovered how to liquify radium, which helped in developing a treatment for cancer. As

a result of his research, he was knighted. MacLennan's family continued to live at 203 William Street after he moved to England. (A plaque behind the house marks the significance of MacLennan.)

During the 1940s, when Princess Juliana of the Netherlands was in Stratford, MacLennan's sisters were invited to entertain her because of their connection to aristocracy. The fact that their brother was knighted made them closer in rank to the princess than any other resident of Stratford.

Retrace your steps and cross to Waterloo Street. Continue north to Mornington Street, noticing the colour of the brick and the different styles of homes.

Sydney-Smith house, 72 Waterloo Street N. (25)

Built in 1866, this Ontario cottage is an early Gothic home once owned by John Sydney-Smith, a local barrister. Sydney-Smith owned the land to the

river and set his house back from the street so that he had an excellent view. As Stratford developed, he sold his land with the stipulation that houses would be set back like his so that his view of the river would not be obscured. This explains why this block has recessed houses. Take a look at the next block and see when this practice changed.

Cross the street and proceed to Mornington.

Gordon House, 198 Mornington Street (26)

The Gordon house was owned and built around 1900 by local merchant William Gordon, the mayor of Stratford when the city incorporated in 1885. Its location at the curve of one of Stratford's main streets attest to Gordon's prominence at the time. It is an excellent example of a Queen Anne revival style building. A later addition transformed the house into a seniors' home.

Monteith Home, 186 Mornington Street (27)

This house was originally an early Italianate home built in 1872, complete with a bay window. It was altered after the turn of the century when a neoclassical portico was added, giving the building a more majestic look. It was owned by the Honourable J. Waldo Monteith, the Minister of Health during the 1960s. Head west.

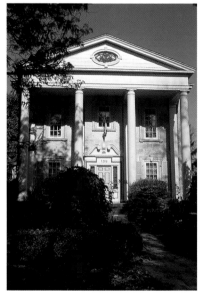

176 Mornington Street (28)

Stratford's connection to Shakespeare is illustrated in this Tudor revival style building constructed in 1928. There aren't many of these houses in Stratford since this style was popular during the 1930s when few people had the money to build them.

Continue to Britannia Street.

2 Britannia Street (29)

This house is an excellent example of Queen Anne revival, built in 1901, with white brick and contrasting materials. It is nicely situated to fit the street and is prominent in this neighbourhood.

Cross to 126 Mornington Street.

126 Mornington Street (30)

This 1879 Italianate style home is complete with ornate brackets. A large two and a half storey building, it cannot be confused with the smaller Gothic Ontario house.

Cross the street and head to 109 and 119 Mornington Street.

109 and 119 Mornington Street (31 and 32)

These are early Italianate homes built about the same time, with some different features. Number 119 has a restored front verandah with an enclosed Stratford porch, introduced by McLagan's furniture factory during the 1880s. It was built in 1888 while 109 was built in 1877.

Continue to Elizabeth Street.

5 Elizabeth Street (33)

Built in 1905, this fine example of Edwardian Classicism was built on the site of the first jail. Notice the height of the building as well as the contrasting detail. It was originally built for a member of the Orr family and again illustrates the family's prosperity.

Head to St. James Church.

46 Mornington Street (34)

Across from St. James Church is a Regency cottage built in two stages, the back part before 1857 and the front part in 1861. It was built for a tinsmith, and the ornate contrasting white brick shows it was an early building.

Continue down the hill to William Street.

Dutch War Memorial (35)

Following World War II, the Dutch government presented Stratford with this monument. The hands are holding an injured bird, which symbolizes Stratford helping the injured Netherlands. It is significant because during World War II, the Dutch army had barracks located in the old McLagan furniture factory, where Dutch soldiers from all over the world were trained.

Continue south.

Plaque Commemorating Stratford's Founding (36)

This plaque marks the location where surveyors and settlers camped before any permanent buildings were constructed. It is also the site where William Berwick stopped people from continuing up the Huron Road during the cholera epidemic in the 1830s.

Continue to the stone bridge.

Stone bridge (37)

The stone bridge was designated as important to Stratford's heritage and has been restored several times. It was designed by architect Alexander Hepburn and built by engineer A. Corrie in 1885.

The two Scotsmen disagreed about many elements of this project, but they did agree on the stone material used to build it.

Cross the street.

Shakespearean Gardens (38)

During the 1920s, R. Thomas Orr suggested that a gardens be built similar to the one in Stratford-upon-Avon, England. It would feature all of the plants mentioned in Shakespeare's plays and be a public park. The Shakespearean Gardens was approved and opened by Governor General Lord Tweedsmuir and his wife Lady Tweedsmuir during an official visit in 1936. It continues to be an important tourist attraction.

Perth County Court House, 1 Huron Street (39)

This building is a fine example of Victorian architecture. Designed in 1885 by George F. Durand, it replaced the first building which was too small. It was built about half an acre away from the jail to avoid past problems with the jail's smell. In 1912, local architect T.J. Hepburn was invited to design a new registry office that would match the courthouse and jail. It is now the home of the Stratford-Perth Archives.

The marker on the front of the courthouse was placed by the Avon Valley Historical Society to recognize John Corrie Wilson Daly's home as the first permanent one in Stratford. Underneath it is a marker for the royal oak, which was planted in 1937 for the coronation of King George VI and Queen Elizabeth.

Continue west on St. Andrew Street.

St. Andrew's Presbyterian Church, 25 St. Andrew Street (40)

St. Andrew's Church was the earliest congregation in Stratford. The present church is a combination of the original church and several Gothic additions added in 1873.

Stratford Public Library, St. Andrew Street (41)

This 1902 building remains one of the oldest Carnegie libraries in Canada. Originally, the main entrance faced St. Andrew Street, but after later additions, it now faces Church Street. This was also the site of Stratford's first school.

Cross the street to the south side of Ontario Street at Church Street.

Festival Square, 10 Downie Street (42)

The Festival Square is comprised of the Gordon Block and the Idington Block. The Gordon Block was built around 1895 and was the first business block in Stratford to use the Chicago style of steel support beams instead of wood. The tower matched the one on Knox Church and the post office that was across from this building. The Idington Block is older and was built by local lawyer, later Supreme Court justice, John Idington, in 1875–1885. The two buildings became known as the Festival Square in the 1970s, after they were threatened to be demolished for a hotel project. They have been designated as heritage buildings.

Continue south to Wellington Street and turn west.

Wellington Street (43)

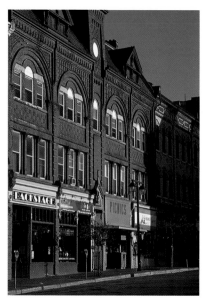

Wellington Street benefitted from being close to the city hall and the railroad. Buildings were named for their owners. These include the Easson Block (1872), the Brandenburger Block (1873) and the Worth Block (1889). All of these blocks were hotels at one time, indicating the importance of Stratford's commercial base and the impact of the railroad.

Conclusion

The tour that you have just taken will ideally whet your appetite for more. Stratford's rich heritage made it difficult to choose which sites to include and which ones to leave out. Nevertheless, we are glad to have been able to introduce you to Stratford's history and we leave you to explore its many other historic sites.

APPENDIX

Stratford Festival Production History
1953–1999

Sir Tyrone Guthrie
Artistic Director (1953–1955)

1953
- *Richard III*
- *All's Well That Ends Well*
- Concerts

1954
- *Measure for Measure*
- *The Taming of the Shrew*
- *Oedipus Rex*
- Concerts

1955
- *Julius Caesar*
- *King Oedipus*
- *The Merchant of Venice*
- *A Soldier's Tale*
- Marcel Marceau
- Concerts

Michael Langham
Artistic Director (1956–1967)

1956
- *Tamburlaine the Great* (tour)
- *Henry V*
- *The Merry Wives of Windsor*
- Three Farces by Molière
  (Le Théâtre du Nouveau Monde)
- *The Rape of Lucretia*

- Concerts
- *Oedipus Rex* (tour)
- *Henry V* (tour)

1957
- *Hamlet*
- *Twelfth Night*
- *The Turn of the Screw*
  (English Opera Group)
- Concerts
- International Film Festival

1958
- *The Broken Jug* (tour)
- *The Two Gentlemen of Verona*
  (tour)
- *Henry IV, Part I*
- *Much Ado About Nothing*
- *Little Carib Dancers*
- *The Winter's Tale*
- Marcel Marceau
- *The Beggar's Opera*
- *Le Malade Imaginaire*
  (Le Théâtre du Nouveau Monde)
- Concerts
- International Film Festival

1959
- *As You Like It*
- *Othello*
- *Orpheus in the Underworld*
- Concerts
- Shakespeare and Music
- International Film Festival

1960
- *King John*
- *A Midsummer Night's Dream*
- *Romeo and Juliet*
- *H.M.S. Pinafore*
- Concerts
- International Film Festival
- *Suite of Psalms for Spoken Voice and Orchestra*
- *The Teacher* (*The Globe and Mail* Stratford Festival Competition)
- *Blind Man's Buff* (*The Globe and Mail* Stratford Festival Competition)
- *H.M.S. Pinafore* (tour)

1961
- *Coriolanus*
- *Henry VIII*
- *Love's Labour's Lost*
- *The Canvas Barricade*
- *The Pirates of Penzance*
- Concerts
- International Film Festival

1962
- Two Programmes of Shakespearean Comedy (tour)
- *Macbeth*
- *The Taming of the Shrew*
- *The Tempest*
- *Cyrano de Bergerac*
- *The Gondoliers*
- Concerts

1963
- *Troilus and Cressida*
- *Cyrano de Bergerac*
- *The Comedy of Errors*
- *Timon of Athens*
- *The Mikado*
- Concerts
- The National Dance Theatre Company of Jamaica

1964
- *Love's Labour's Lost* (tour)
- *Le Bourgeois Gentilhomme* (tour)
- *Timon of Athens* (tour)
- *Richard II*
- *Le Bourgeois Gentilhomme*
- *King Lear*
- *The Country Wife*
- *The Yeomen of the Guard*
- *The Marriage of Figaro*
- Concerts

1965
- *The National Ballet of Canada*
- *Henry IV (Henry IV, Part I)*
- *Falstaff (Henry IV, Part II)*
- *Julius Caesar*
- *The Cherry Orchard*
- *The Rise and Fall of the City of*
- *Mahagonny*
- *The Marriage of Figaro*
- Concerts

1966
- *Henry V*
- *Henry VI*
- *Twelfth Night*
- *The Last of the Tsars*
- *The Dance of Death*
- *Don Giovanni*
- Concerts
- *Rose Latulippe* (Royal Winnipeg Ballet)

1967
- *The Government Inspector* (tour)
- *Twelfth Night* (tour)

- *Richard III*
- *The Government Inspector*
- *The Merry Wives of Windsor*
- *Colours in the Dark*
- *Antony and Cleopatra*
- *Cosi Fan Tutte*
- *Albert Herring*
- Concerts
- *Antony and Cleopatra* (tour)
- *The Government Inspector* (tour)

Jean Gascon
Executive Artistic Director (1968–1969)
Artistic Director (1969–1974)

1968
- *A Midsummer Night's Dream* (tour)
- *A Midsummer Night's Dream*
- *Romeo and Juliet*
- *Tartuffe*
- *The Three Musketeers*
- *The Seagull*
- *Waiting for Godot*
- *Cinderella (La Cenerentola)*
- Concerts
- Royal Winnipeg Ballet

1969
- *The Alchemist* (tour)
- *Hamlet* (tour)
- *Hamlet*
- *The Alchemist*
- *Measure for Measure*
- *Tartuffe*
- *Hadrian VII*
- *Hadrian VII* (tour)
- *The Satyricon*

- Concerts
- *Hamlet* (tour)
- *The Alchemist* (tour)
- *Sauerkringle* (Ottawa)
- *Bust Out* (School tour)
- *Four Plays by Jean-Claude van Itallie* (Ottawa)

1970
- *The Hostage* (Ottawa)
- *The Empire Builders* (Ottawa)
- *The Merchant of Venice* (tour)
- *The School for Scandal* (tour)
- *As You Like It* (School tour)
- Three Plays by Mrozek
- *The Merchant of Venice*
- *The School for Scandal*
- *Hedda Gabler*
- *The Sun Never Sets*
- *The Architect and the Emperor of Assyria*
- *Cymbeline*
- *The Friends*
- *Vatzlav*
- Marcel Marceau
- Concerts
- *Cymbeline* (tour)
- *Tartuffe* (tour)

1971
- *Much Ado About Nothing* (tour)
- *The Duchess of Malfi* (tour)
- *Much Ado About Nothing*
- *The Duchess of Malfi*
- *Macbeth*
- *An Italian Straw Hat*
- *The Red Convertible*
- *Volpone*
- *There's One in Every Marriage*

- The Montreal Marionettes
- America's National Theatre of Puppet Arts
- Adrian Pecknold's Canadian Mime Theatre
- Concerts
- International Film Festival

1972
- *There's One in Every Marriage* (New York)
- *As You Like It* (tour)
- *Lorenzaccio* (tour)
- *As You Like It*
- *Lorenzaccio*
- *King Lear*
- *The Threepenny Opera*
- *Orpheus*
- *Mark*
- *She Stoops to Conquer*
- *Pinocchio*
- *La Guerre, Yes Sir!*
- *Patria II: Requiems for the Party Girl*
- Concerts
- Music for a Summer Day
- International Film Festival

1973
- *The Taming of the Shrew* (European tour)
- *King Lear* (European tour)
- *The Taming of the Shrew*
- *She Stoops to Conquer*
- *Othello*
- *A Month in the Country*
- *The Collected Works of Billy the Kid*
- *Pericles*
- *Inook and the Sun*
- *The Marriage Brokers*

- *Exiles*
- Concerts
- International Film Festival

1974
- *The Imaginary Invalid* (Australian tour)
- *The Imaginary Invalid*
- *Pericles*
- *Love's Labour's Lost*
- *La Vie Parisienne*
- *The Summoning of Everyman*
- *The Medium*
- *King John*
- *Walsh*
- *Ready Steady Go*
- Concerts
- International Film Festival

Robin Phillips
Artistic Director (1975–1980)

1975
- *The Two Gentlemen of Verona* (tour)
- *The Comedy of Errors* (tour)
- *Saint Joan*
- *The Comedy of Errors*
- *Twelfth Night*
- *Measure for Measure*
- *The Two Gentlemen of Verona*
- *The Crucible*
- *Trumpets and Drums*
- *The Fool*
- *Le Magicien*
- *Ariadne auf Naxos*
- *Fellowship*
- *Oscar Remembered*
- *Kennedy's Children*

- *The Importance of Being Earnest*
- Concerts
- International Film Festival

1976
- *The Tempest* (tour)
- *Hamlet* (tour)
- *Hamlet*
- *The Way of the World*
- *The Merchant of Venice*
- *The Tempest*
- *Antony and Cleopatra*
- *The Importance of Being Earnest*
- *Measure for Measure*
- *Eve*
- *A Midsummer Night's Dream*
- *Three Sisters*
- Concerts

1977
- *A Midsummer Night's Dream*
- *Romeo and Juliet*
- *All's Well That Ends Well*
- *Ghosts*
- *Miss Julie*
- *Richard III*
- *The Guardsman*
- *Much Ado About Nothing*
- *As You Like It*
- *Hay Fever*
- Concerts

1978
- A Gala Shakespeare Revel
- *The Merry Wives of Windsor*
- *The Devils*
- *Macbeth*
- *Uncle Vanya*
- *Candide*
- *The Winter's Tale*

- *As You Like It*
- *Judgement*
- *Heloise and Abelard: Love Letters from the Middle Ages*
- *Ned and Jack*
- *Medea*
- *Private Lives*
- *Julius Caesar*
- Four Plays by Samuel Beckett
- *Stargazing*
- *Titus Andronicus*
- Concerts

1979
- Gala Performance
- *Love's Labour's Lost*
- *Ned and Jack*
- *The First Part of Henry IV*
- *Richard II*
- *The Importance of Being Earnest*
- *The Second Part of Henry IV*
- *Happy New Year*
- *The Taming of the Shrew*
- *The Woman*
- *Othello*
- *Victoria*
- *Barren / Yerma*
- *King Lear*
- Concerts

1980
- *The Beggar's Opera*
- *Twelfth Night*
- *Henry V*
- *Virginia*
- *The Servant of Two Masters*
- *Titus Andronicus*
- *The Gin Game*
- *Much Ado About Nothing*

- *Bosoms and Neglect*
- *Brief Lives*
- *Foxfire*
- *The Seagull*
- *Henry VI*
- *King Lear*
- *Long Day's Journey into Night*
- Stratford Youth Choir

John Hirsch
Associate Artistic Director (1968–1969)
Artistic Director (1981–1985)

1981
- *Virginia* (tour)
- *The Misanthrope*
- *H.M.S. Pinafore*
- *Coriolanus*
- *The Taming of the Shrew*
- *The Rivals*
- *The Comedy of Errors*
- *The Visit*
- *Wild Oats*
- Concerts
- *Wild Oats* (Ottawa)

1982
- *Julius Caesar*
- *The Mikado*
- *The Merry Wives of Windsor*
- *The Tempest*
- *Letters of Love and Affection*
- *A Midsummer Night's Dream*
- *All's Well That Ends Well*
- *Translations*
- *Damien*
- *Arms and the Man*
- *Mary Stuart*
- *A Variable Passion*

- *Blithe Spirit*
- Concerts
- *Translations* (Ottawa)
- *Blithe Spirit* (Toronto)
- *The Mikado* (Ottawa)

1983
- *Translations* (Toronto)
- *Macbeth*
- *The Gondoliers*
- *As You Like It*
- *Richard II*
- *Blake*
- *Damien*
- *The Mikado*
- *When That I Was...*
- *Irene Worth: Virtuoso Performances*
- *The Country Wife*
- *Tartuffe*
- *Love's Labour's Lost*
- *Much Ado About Nothing*
- *Death of a Salesman*
- Concerts
- *The Gondoliers* (tour)
- *The Mikado* (tour)
- *A Variable Passion* (tour)

1984
- *A Midsummer Night's Dream*
- *Iolanthe*
- *Romeo and Juliet*
- *Love's Labour's Lost*
- *The Gondoliers*
- *Waiting for Godot*
- *The Two Gentlemen of Verona*
- *The Mikado*
- *Tartuffe*
- *Henry IV, Part I*
- *The Merchant of Venice*

- *A Streetcar Named Desire*
- *Iolanthe* (tour)
- *Separate Tables*
- Concerts
- *Separate Tables* (Toronto)

1985
- *King Lear*
- *The Pirates of Penzance*
- *Twelfth Night*
- *Measure for Measure*
- *Antigone*
- *The Beaux Stratagem*
- *She Stoops to Conquer*
- *The Government Inspector*
- *The Glass Menagerie*
- Concerts
- *King Lear* (U.S. tour)
- *Twelfth Night* (U.S. tour)

John Neville
Artistic Director (1986–1989)

1986
- *The Boys from Syracuse*
- *Hamlet*
- *The Winter's Tale*
- *Rosencrantz and Guildenstern are Dead*
- *Pericles*
- *Henry VIII*
- *The Resistible Rise of Arturo Ui*
- *Macbeth*
- *A Man for All Seasons*
- *Cymbeline*
- Concerts
- *Macbeth* (tour)
- *A Man for All Seasons* (Ottawa)

1987
- *Cabaret*
- *Nora*
- *Mother Courage*
- *As You Like It*
- *Troilus and Cressida*
- *The School for Scandal*
- *The Cherry Orchard*
- *Romeo and Juliet*
- *Not About Heroes*
- *Intimate Admiration*
- *Journey's End*
- *Othello*
- *Much Ado About Nothing*

1988
- *Richard III*
- *All's Well That Ends Well*
- *The Taming of the Shrew*
- *Twelfth Night*
- *Murder in the Cathedral*
- *My Fair Lady*
- *King Lear*
- *The Two Gentlemen of Verona*
- *Not About Heroes*
- *The Three Musketeers*
- *Irma La Douce*
- *Oedipus / The Critic*
- *The Two Gentlemen of Verona* (tour)

1989
- *Titus Andronicus / The Comedy of Errors*
- *A Midsummer Night's Dream*
- *The Merchant of Venice*
- *Three Sisters*
- *Kiss Me Kate*
- *Henry V*
- *Love's Labour's Lost*
- *The Changeling*

- *The Shoemakers' Holiday*
- *The Relapse*
- *The Proposal*
- *Cat on a Hot Tin Roof*
- *Guthrie on Guthrie*
- *The Lunatic, The Lover & The Poet*

David William
Artistic Director (1990–1993)

1990
- *Macbeth*
- *The Merry Wives of Windsor*
- *As You Like It*
- *Home*
- *Guys & Dolls*
- *Love for Love*
- *Memoir*
- *Forever Yours, Marie-Lou*
- *Phaedra*
- *Julius Caesar*
- *The Knight of the Burning Pestle*
- *Ah, Wilderness!*
- *The Lunatic, The Lover & The Poet*
- *The Grand Inquisitor/Swan Song*
- *One Tiger to a Hill*
- *Love for Love* (tour)
- *Phaedra* (Dartmouth College)

1991
- *Hamlet*
- *Our Town*
- *Much Ado About Nothing*
- *Twelfth Night*
- *Carousel*
- *Les Belles Soeurs*
- *Timon of Athens*
- *Homeward Bound*
- *The Rules of the Game*

- *Treasure Island*
- *The Knight of the Burning Pestle*
- *The School for Wives*
- *Love Letters*
- *An Enemy of the People*

1992
- *The Tempest*
- *Romeo and Juliet*
- *Love's Labour's Lost*
- *Measure for Measure*
- *World of Wonders*
- *H.M.S. Pinafore*
- *Entertaining Mr. Sloane*
- *The Wingfield Trilogy*
- *Uncle Vanya*
- *Bonjour, là, Bonjour*
- *Shirley Valentine*
- *The Two Gentlemen of Verona*
- Words and Music Concert Series

1993
- *Antony and Cleopatra*
- *King John*
- *A Midsummer Night's Dream*
- *Gypsy*
- *The Wingfield Trilogy*
- *Bacchae*
- *The Mikado*
- *Fair Liberty's Call*
- *The Importance of Being Earnest*
- *The Imaginary Invalid*
- *The Illusion*
- Words and Music Concert Series
- *The Importance of Being Earnest* (Ann Arbor)
- *A Midsummer Night's Dream* (Ann Arbor)

Richard Monette
Artistic Director Designate (1992–1993)
Artistic Director (1994–Present)

1994
- *Twelfth Night*
- *Long Day's Journey into Night*
- *The Pirates of Penzance*
- *Hamlet*
- *Cyrano de Bergerac*
- *In the Ring*
- *Othello*
- *Alice Through the Looking Glass*
- *The Comedy of Errors*
- *Husbands and Cuckolds*

1995
- *The Merry Wives of Windsor*
- *The Boy Friend*
- *Macbeth*
- *The Gondoliers*
- *The Country Wife*
- *Long Day's Journey into Night*
- *The Comedy of Errors*
- *Amadeus*
- *The Stillborn Lover*

1996
- *King Lear*
- *The Music Man*
- *Amadeus*
- *The Little Foxes*
- *A Fitting Confusion*
- *The Merchant of Venice*
- *Alice Through the Looking Glass*
- *Barrymore*
- *As You Like It*
- *Sweet Bird of Youth*
- *Waiting for Godot*

1997
- *Camelot*
- *The Taming of the Shrew*
- *Romeo and Juliet*
- *Oedipus Rex*
- *Death of a Salesman*
- *Little Women*
- *Filumena*
- *Equus*
- *Richard III*
- *Juno and the Paycock*
- *Coriolanus*
- *Wingfield Unbound*

1998
- *Julius Caesar*
- *Man of La Mancha*
- *A Man for All Seasons* (tour)
- *The Two Gentlemen of Verona*
- *The Prime of Miss Jean Brodie*
- *Much Ado About Nothing* (tour)
- *The Miracle Worker*
- *The Miser* (tour)
- *The Winter's Tale*
- *The Cherry Orchard*
- *The Night of the Iguana*
- *Waiting for Godot*

1999
- *The Tempest*
- *A Midsummer Night's Dream*
- *Pride and Prejudice*
- *The Alchemist*
- *The School for Scandal*
- *West Side Story*
- *Dracula*
- *Richard II*
- *Macbeth*
- *Glenn*

BIBLIOGRAPHY

Archival Sources

Stratford Festival Archives. Series of records and programs of the Stratford Shakespearean
Festival.

Stratford-Perth Archives. Various series of records,
research files, scrapbooks, manuscript col-
lections, photographs.

Bibliography

Anderson, James. *Stratford Library Services Since 1846.*
Stratford: Stratford Public Library, 1975.

City of Stratford. *1994 Annual Report on Economic
Activity.* Stratford: City of Stratford, 1995.

Coleman, Thelma. *The Canada Company.* Stratford:
County of Perth and Cumming Publishers,
1978.

———. *Stratford, The City Beautiful: The Story of the
Stratford and District Horticultural Society
1878–1978.* Stratford: Canadian
Household Advertising Ltd., 1978.

Davies, Robertson, Tyrone Guthrie, Tanya
Moiseiwitsch, Boyd Neel. *Thrice the Brinded
Cat Hath Mew'd.* Canada: Clarke, Irwin and
Company, 1955.

Edmonds, Jane. "An Economic Analysis of the
Stratford Festival." Unpublished article in
the Stratford Festival Archives, 1989.

Gaines, Robert A. *John Neville Takes Command: The Story
of the Stratford Shakespearean Festival in Production.*
Stratford: William Street Press, 1987.

Good, Maurice. *Every Inch a Lear: A Rehearsal Journal.*
Victoria: n.p. 1982.

Guthrie, Tyrone. *A Life in the Theatre.* London:
Hamish Hamilton Ltd., 1959. Reprint.
London: Readers Union Hamish
Hamilton, 1961. Reprint. New York:
Proscenium Publishers Inc.,

Guthrie, Tyrone, Robertson Davies and Grant
Macdonald. *Renown at Stratford.* Toronto:
Clarke, Irwin & Company Ltd., 1953.

———, Robertson Davies and Grant Macdonald.
*Twice Have the Trumpets Sounded: A Record of
the Stratford Shakespearean Festival in Canada,
1954.* Toronto: Clarke, Irwin &
Company Ltd., 1954.

Johnston, William. *History of the County of Perth from
1825 to 1902.* Stratford: County of Perth,
1903. Reprint. Stratford: County of Perth,
1976.

Bibliography

Johnston, W. Stafford. *The Fighting Perths.* Stratford: Perth Regiment Veterans Association, 1964.

Johnston, W. Stafford and Hugh J. M. Johnston. *History of Perth County to 1967.* Stratford: County of Perth 1967.

Knelman, Martin. *A Stratford Tempest.* Toronto: n.p. 1982.

Leitch, Adelaide. *Floodtides of Fortune.* Stratford: The Corporation of the City of Stratford, 1980.

Lennon, Mary Jane. *A Stratford Album: Memories of the Festival City.* Erin: The Boston Mills Press, 1985.

Lizars, Kathleen and Robina MacFarlane. *In the Days of the Canada Company.* Toronto: William Briggs, 1896. Reprint. Toronto: Coles Publishing Company, 1972.

MacFarlane, Richard Nelson. "Social Impact of Tourism: Resident Attitudes in Stratford." Unpublished M.A. thesis, University of Western Ontario, London, 1979.

Miller, Robert J. *The Swans of Stratford.* Stratford: author, 1995.

Monsarrat, Nicholas. *To Stratford with Love.* Toronto: McClelland and Stewart, 1963.

Morton, Desmond. "Aid to the Civil Power: The Stratford Strike of 1933" in *On Strike: Six Key Labour Struggles in Canada 1919–1949,* edited by Irving Arabella, 79–91. Toronto: James Lorimer & Company, 1975.

Ontario Ministry of Industry and Tourism. *Stratford Festival Survey,* 1972. Toronto: n.p. 1972.

Patterson, Tom and Allan Gould. *First Stage: The Making of the Stratford Festival.* Toronto: McClelland and Stewart, 1987.

Pettigrew, John and Jamie Portman. *Stratford: The First Thirty Years.* 2 vols. Toronto: Macmillan of Canada, 1985.

Raby, Peter, comp. and ed., *The Stratford Scene 1958–1968.* Toronto: Clarke, Irwin & Company Ltd.

Reid, Barbara and Thelma Morrison. *A Star Danced: The Story of How Stratford Started the Stratford Festival.* Toronto: Robert Reid, 1994.

Robinson, Dean. *Railway Stratford.* Erin: Boston Mills Press, 1989.

———. *Reflections: A History of the Stratford Agricultural Society 1841–1991.* Stratford: Stratford Agricultural Society, 1991.

Robinson, Dean. *Y Stratford: A History 1858–1991.* Stratford: Willow Run Publications, 1991.

Saddlemyer, Ann and Richard Plant, eds. *Later Stages: Essays in Ontario Theatre from the First World War to the 1970s.* Toronto: University of Toronto Press, 1997.

Shaw, Grace Lydiatt. *Stratford Under Cover: Memories on Tape*. Toronto: N. C. Press Ltd. 1977.

Somerset, J. Alan B. *The Stratford Festival Story. A Catalogue-Index to the Stratford, Ontario Festival, 1953–1990*. New York: Greenwood Press, 1991.

Stratford Beacon. "Old Boys' Reunion Special Editions" in *Stratford Beacon*. Stratford: Stratford Beacon, 1906, 1914, 1932, 1953.

Stratford Economic Development. *Stratford Industrial Directory, 1995*. Stratford: City of Stratford, 1995.

Stratford-Perth Archives. "Reflections" series in *Beacon Herald*. Stratford: Beacon Herald, 1988–1998.

Stratford Shakespearean Festival Foundation. *The Stratford Story*. Stratford: n. p. 1954 and 1955

Stratford Weekly Beacon. Stratford: Stratford Beacon (1855–1900). Microfilm at Stratford-Perth Archives.

Stratford Beacon Herald. Stratford: Beacon Fine Printing. Microfilm at Stratford-Perth Archives.

Strickland, Samuel. *Twenty-Seven Years in Canada West*. London: 1853. Reprint. Edmonton: M. G. Hurtig Ltd., 1970.

The Stratford Festival 1953–1957. Toronto: Clarke, Irwin & Company Ltd., 1958.

Thomas, Harold M. "Research on Sports in Stratford." Unpublished manuscript located at Stratford-Perth Archives, 1995.318.

INDEX

Photo Credits

Key: T = Top, C = Centre, B = Bottom

Bracketed names are the photographers'.

Images on the following pages appear courtesy of the individuals and institutions noted below. All other photographs were taken by Terry Manzo and are the property of the publisher.

Evans, Steven: 11B; London Museum of Archaeology: 13T&B, 14; Stratford Festival Archives: 5C (Terry Manzo), 6 (Cylla von Tiedemann), 56 (Kerry Hayes), 57, 58T, 58B (Richard Bain), 59T, 59B (Peter Smith), 61T (present at photo session but not shown: Michael Bates, Norman Roland and George Alexander), 61B (Peter Smith), 62, 63 (Terry Manzo), 64B (Terry Manzo), 65 (Cylla von Tiedemann; *The Two Gentleman of Verona* by William Shakespeare: directed by Richard Rose; set design by Teresa Przybylski; costume design by Charlotte Dean; lighting design by Kevin Fraser; music composed by Don Horsburgh; sound design by Jim Neil; fight direction by James Binkley), 66T (Cylla von Tiedemann; *The Mikado* by W.S. Gilbert and Arthur Sullivan: directed and choreographed by Brian Macdonald; musical direction and additional arrangements by Berthold Carriere; designed by Susan Benson; lighting designed by Michael J. Whitfield;consulting direction and choreography by Anne Wootten; additional lyrics by John Banks), 66B (Peter Smith); Stratford Public Library: 16; Stratford-Perth Archives: 4B, 18T, 19, 20T, 24, 26T, 27T&B, 29, 30T, 31, 33, 35B, 36, 37, 38, 39B, 40T&B, 41T&B, 42T, 43, 44, 47, 49, 50, 60; Tourism Stratford: 5B; U.S. Department of the Interior (Edison National Historic Site): 28; Wishart, Scott: 3

The items on 20B, 22T&B, 26C&B, 30B, 39T, 42B come from the collection of the Stratford-Perth Museum and on 45T&B, 46 from Art Boon.

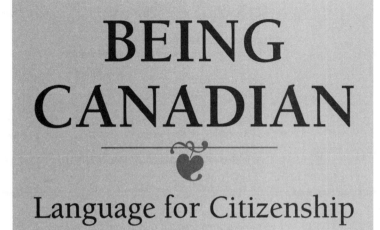

BEING CANADIAN

Language for Citizenship

Judy Cameron

Tracey M. Derwing

Prentice Hall Regents Canada
Scarborough, Ontario

Canadian Cataloguing in Publication Data

Cameron, Judy, 1953–
Being Canadian : language for citizenship

Includes index.
ISBN 0–13–447319–1

1. Readers (Adult). 2. Readers — Canada.
3. Readers — Citizenship — Canada. 4. English language —
   Textbooks for second language learners.
5. Citizenship — Canada. I. Derwing, Tracey Mary, 1951–.II. Title.

PE1126.N43C3 1996   428.6'4   C95–931391–5

Prentice-Hall, Inc., Englewood Cliffs, New Jersey
Prentice-Hall International (UK) Limited, London
Prentice-Hall of Australia, Pty. Limited, Sydney
Prentice-Hall Hispanoamericana, S.A., Mexico City
Prentice-Hall of India Private Limited, New Delhi
Prentice-Hall of Japan, Inc., Tokyo
Simon & Schuster Asia Private Limited, Singapore
Editora Prentice-Hall do Brasil, Ltda., Rio de Janeiro

ISBN 0–13–447319–1

Executive Editor: Clifford J. Newman
Managing Editor: Marta Tomins
Production Editor: Imogen Brian
Production Coordinator: Sharon Houston
Cover/Interior Design: Monica Kompter
Cover Images: Anthony de Ridder; Government of Canada
Page Layout: Joan Morrison

1 2 3 4 5 W 00 99 98 97 96

Printed and bound in Canada

This book is dedicated to our friend, Murray Munro

Table of Contents

Preface

Being Canadian is a reader suitable for students in LINC or other ESL programs where Canadian content is mandatory. Using a topical approach, the book covers the themes of social, cultural, and political history; physical and political geography; the structure of the Parliamentary system and the electoral process; and the nature of the economy. In recognition of the fact that citizenship resources are often difficult for instructors to obtain, a list of inexpensive or free resources is provided at the end of the book.

Traditionally, citizenship materials have focused on geography, history, government, and rights and responsibilities. *Being Canadian* covers these topics and shows the relationship among each of these areas, current situations, and the students' own lives. The contact activities in each chapter encourage students to apply their knowledge and skills outside the classroom, to become aware of and involved in community affairs, and to develop ties with people from a variety of cultural backgrounds.

One unique feature of *Being Canadian* is its inclusion of sensitive issues and immigrant viewpoints. The authors' own experience as ESL and citizenship instructors has made it clear that adult immigrants want to address both the positive and the negative aspects of an issue.

The chapters are designed as self-contained units; that is, it is not necessary to read them in any particular order. Furthermore, any chapter can be used as a supplement to other texts in ESL classrooms. Each unit in *Being Canadian* contains realistic, captioned illustrations and photographs directly related to the text.

At the end of each chapter there is a self-test section where students can test their knowledge of the material covered in the unit. Additionally, there is a practice test at the end of the book that deals with issues and knowledge covered throughout the book (Canadian geography, history and government, and the rights and responsibilities of Canadian citizenship). Answer keys are provided.

FORMAT OF THE BOOK

The book contains 12 Chapters which follow a similar format. Chapter 13 is a practice test. The general organization of each chapter is as follows:

MATERIALS REQUIRED/SKILLS EMPHASIZED

These sections tell the instructor what materials will be needed (for example, a map, telephone directory) and which skills to emphasize (for example, reading, constructing a graph).

PRE-READINGS

This section prepares students for the readings ahead. The pre-reading usually involves a graphic (charts, photos, flow diagrams, etc.) and accompanying questions (advanced organizers, general discussion questions, etc.). This is an opportunity for the teacher to determine the degree of knowledge that the students have and to build necessary vocabulary and concepts prior to doing the readings.

READINGS

A basic introduction to the topic.

COMPREHENSION AND DISCUSSION QUESTIONS

This section presents comprehension questions that assess students' understanding of the reading, and discussion questions that draw from students' own experiences, backgrounds, and beliefs.

LANGUAGE AND CONTACT ACTIVITIES

This section contains a variety of activities designed to reinforce the knowledge gained in the reading passage. It also develops language skills and citizenship participation. Students are required to make lists, rank order items, describe, compare and contrast, make choices, evaluate ideas, develop generalizations, solve problems, read graphs, etc. Contact exercises serve to engage students with their communities. For example, in Chapter 6, *Canada Today: A Multicultural Society,* students develop a survey of people's attitudes towards immigration. They interview people and then compile, analyze, and discuss their results.

CANADIAN ISSUE

Each chapter focuses on at least one interesting Canadian issue related to the main topic. Many of the issues give the instructor an opportunity to address sensitive topics.

SIDEBARS

Most chapters contain one or more sidebars which provide interesting information related to the main topic.

GLOSSARY

For each chapter, a glossary of new or difficult terms is provided.

TEST YOURSELF

Each chapter ends with test questions on the content covered in the unit. Answer keys are provided.

TEACHING TIPS

- Each chapter includes a glossary of new vocabulary. Of course, there will be other words that students do not know. As they come across new or difficult words, ask the students to add the new words and their definitions to the vocabulary list at the back of each chapter.

- Many students appreciate listening to the readings on their own. You may want to record the readings onto audio tape for the students.

- Graded newspapers (*East Coast Reader, Welcome News, Ontario Times, English Express, and West Coast Reader*) often cover topics that are related to issues in this book. Class sets are usually available through your provincial government.

- End-of-chapter reviews may be helpful for the students. Spelling bees, matching vocabulary with definitions, and content questions all help the students remember what they have learned.

ACKNOWLEDGEMENTS

We began teaching citizenship classes in 1982. Little did we know what a continuing impact that first course would have. Much of the material in this book stems from our own experiences and those of our colleagues and students. We are particularly grateful to Jeff Bullard, Pat Dunne, Hilary Hellum, Jenny Maloney, and Wendy Rollins for the spirit of collaboration in which they shared their ideas for teaching citizenship concepts, so long ago. We would also like to acknowledge the National Working Group on Citizenship Education who contributed significantly to our view of participatory citizenship.

There are many people who provided assistance in the development of this text. Several experienced ESL instructors read earlier versions and provided helpful suggestions for improvement. Liz Karra, Dean MacKay, Murray McMahon, Murray Munro, Albert Penner, Georgia Ramos, and Siegi Solti all gave useful input. A special thanks goes to Fiona Sime for piloting sections of the book in her ESL class.

We are indebted to Doug Engel for the artistic graphics he produced. The following individuals assisted with photographs: Jeff Bullard, Sarah Cameron, Kelly Robart, Janet Schwegel, and Ron Smyth.

We would also like to thank Jim Critchley of Alberta Vocational College, Edmonton for generously allowing us access to the college's LINC curriculum, and for giving us a chance to meet and interview ESL students on issues related to citizenship. Thanks to Jerome Hendricks and other AVC staff for their openness.

Finally, we acknowledge the incredible students we have met over the years. We feel proud that we contributed in some way to their becoming Canadian citizens.

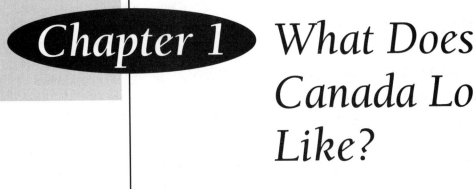

Chapter 1 *What Does Canada Look Like?*

MATERIALS REQUIRED A large world map, a large map of Canada, a map of your province or territory, an atlas, several maps of your city, and pictures from various regions of Canada to supplement the readings. In addition, ask students to bring photos of their native country and currency from their country.

SKILLS EMPHASIZED Reading comprehension, discussion, conducting a survey, expressing an opinion, making choices, comparing, identifying, classifying, describing, map reading, letter writing, listening.

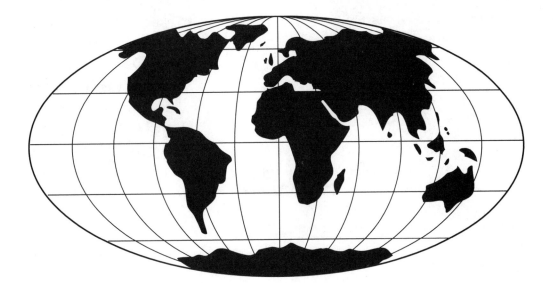

PRE-READING I

In a group, answer the following questions:

🕭 What country are you from? Find your country on a world map.

🕭 What city or town are you from? Find it on a world map.

🕭 Who comes from the smallest country?

VIOLET CHAN'S TRIP TO CANADA

Violet Chan came to Canada on June 18, 1994. She flew from Hong Kong to Vancouver. After two days in Vancouver, she flew to Winnipeg. Her brother met her at the airport and drove her to his apartment in Brandon, Manitoba.

Graphic: Doug Engel

- Who comes from the largest country?
- Who traveled the farthest to get to Canada? Whose trip took the longest?
- Find Hong Kong, Vancouver, Winnipeg and Brandon on a map.
- Draw your journey to Canada.
- Tell your story to a partner by answering these questions:

  When did you come to Canada?

  How did you get here?

  Where did you go first?

  Then where did you go?

  How did you feel when you arrived in Canada?

  Did you come alone?

  Why did you come to Canada?

  What did you know about Canada before you came here?

  What surprised you most about Canada?

- Write a paragraph about your journey to Canada. The teacher will read the students' paragraphs aloud. Guess who wrote each paragraph.

READING I: CANADA

Canada is the second largest country in the world but it has a very small population. *1* There are only about 27 million people in the whole country. Most people live in the south and central parts of Canada. Very few people live in the north. In fact, 75 percent (75%) of Canadians live within 160 kilometres of the Canada–United States (US) border. Canada has oceans on three sides: the Pacific in the west, the Atlantic in the east, and the Arctic in the north.

Canada is made up of ten provinces and two territories. The capital of *2* Canada is Ottawa, Ontario. The Canadian (federal) government is there. Each province and territory also has a capital city. The provincial governments are in the capital cities.

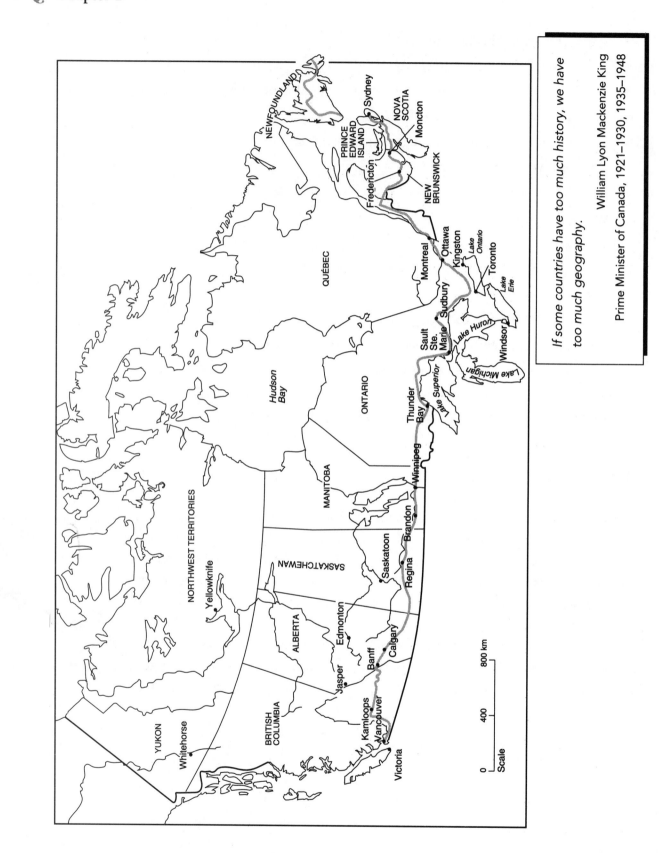

If some countries have too much history, we have too much geography.

William Lyon Mackenzie King
Prime Minister of Canada, 1921–1930, 1935–1948

PROVINCES, TERRITORIES, AND CAPITAL CITIES

Province/Territory	Capital City
British Columbia (B.C. or BC)	Victoria
Alberta (Alta. or AB)	Edmonton
Saskatchewan (Sask. or SK)	Regina
Manitoba (Man. or MB)	Winnipeg
Ontario (Ont. or ON)	Toronto
Quebec (Que. or PQ)	Quebec City
New Brunswick (N.B. or NB)	Fredericton
Nova Scotia (N.S. or NS)	Halifax
Prince Edward Island (P.E.I. or PE)	Charlottetown
Newfoundland (Nfld. or NF)	St. John's
Northwest Territories (N.W.T. or NT)	Yellowknife
Yukon (Y.T. or YK)	Whitehorse

COMPREHENSION AND DISCUSSION QUESTIONS

1. Canada is the second largest country in the world. What is the largest country? (Is it Russia, the United States or Australia?)
2. What is the population of Canada?
3. What is the population of the country you come from?
4. Where do most Canadians live?
5. What countries or oceans are on Canada's borders?
6. What city is the capital of Canada?
7. What city is the capital of your country?
8. Which province do you live in? What is the capital?

LANGUAGE AND CONTACT ACTIVITIES

1. Map Reading

Using a map of Canada, locate:

- the ten provinces and the two territories
- the capital of each province

- the capital cities of the territories
- the capital of Canada
- the biggest province
- the smallest province
- the three oceans
- Hudson Bay

2. Giving and Following Directions

In pairs, look at a map of your city. Choose a place you would like to go to and write it down on a piece of paper. Don't show your partner. Give your partner directions to the place starting from his/her house. Once your partner has found the place you chose, listen to directions to the place your partner chose.

3. Comparing Canada to Your Country of Origin

In groups, answer the following questions:

- Which country is bigger, Canada or your first country?
- Which country has a larger population, Canada or your first country?
- Which is the largest city in your first country?
- What type of government is in power in the country you come from?
- Is the place where you live now bigger or smaller than where you lived in your first country?
- What languages are spoken in your first country?

4. Facts About Canada and Your Country

On the chart on page 7, fill in information about your country.

- Show your classmates some money from your country. What is the value of your currency in Canadian money?
- Put photos of your country around the room. Once all the students have put up pictures, guess which country each of the photos is from. Do any of the pictures look like places you have seen in Canada?

	CANADA	YOUR COUNTRY OF ORIGIN
Official Languages	English & French	
Population	Small — 27 000 000 people	
Largest City	Toronto	
Government	Parliamentary democracy	
Currency	Canadian dollar	
Weather/Seasons	Hot in summer, cold in winter; 4 seasons	
Size	Second largest country in the world (9 970 000 sq. km)	

PRE-READING II

In pairs:

🍂 Locate the Trans Canada Highway on a road map of Canada.

🍂 What cities are on the Trans Canada Highway between Vancouver and Banff?

🍂 Find the Great Lakes — what are their names?

🍂 Find Thunder Bay and Sudbury in Ontario.

🍂 Find Ottawa, Montreal and Toronto. Find Moncton and Sydney.

🍂 Every map has a legend which tells you how to read the map. For example, most maps show how to measure the distance between two places. Using the map of Canada, find out how far it is from

Winnipeg to Regina	Toronto to Montreal
Calgary to Edmonton	Halifax to Fredericton
Ottawa to Montreal	Whitehorse to Yellowknife

🍂 If you drove at 100 kilometres per hour, how long would it take to go from

Montreal to Quebec City?	Calgary to Winnipeg?
Thunder Bay to Sudbury?	Vancouver to Kamloops?
Saskatoon to Regina?	

The Vancouver Harbour Seabus carries passengers into downtown Vancouver, B.C., Canada's third largest city

Moraine Lake and the Valley of the Ten Peaks is located in the heart of the Rockies

Government of Canada

Government of Canada

READING II: A TRIP ACROSS CANADA

1   The Trans Canada Highway is the longest national road in the world (7821 kilometres). You can travel all the way from Victoria, British Columbia to St. John's, Newfoundland. Victoria, the capital of British Columbia, is on Vancouver Island. Victoria is one of the warmest places in Canada — it has mild winters and there are flowers almost all year round. To go from Victoria to Vancouver, you take a ferry. After a one-and-a-half-hour boat ride, passing many small islands, you arrive in Vancouver, the third-largest Canadian city. Vancouver is surrounded by mountains and the Pacific ocean. Many people think it is one of the most beautiful cities in the world.

Visitors come from all over the world to see the rodeo events at the Calgary Stampede

Provincial Archives of Alberta

After driving all day through mountains in British Columbia, you will arrive in Banff, Alberta. Banff is located in the heart of the Rocky Mountains. Tourists from all over the world come to visit Banff and Jasper National Parks. In the winter they ski, and in the summer they camp and hike. From Banff the Trans Canada Highway goes through the foothills into the city of Calgary. Calgary is famous for its rodeo, the Calgary Stampede.

After leaving Calgary, the highway goes through the Prairies in Alberta, Saskatchewan and Manitoba. After a day of driving through wheat fields, you arrive in Regina, the capital of Saskatchewan. Another day on the road brings you to Winnipeg, Manitoba. Some people don't like the Prairies because much of the land is flat, but Prairie people love the wide open spaces and the huge blue sky.

Just east of Winnipeg on the Trans Canada Highway is a region of rocks and trees. By the time you reach Ontario the road starts to twist and turn for hundreds of kilometres. The first big city on the Trans Canada in Ontario is Thunder Bay. Thunder Bay is on Lake Superior, one of the five Great Lakes. The Highway follows the lakeshore to Sault Ste. Marie where Lake Huron meets Lake Superior. From there, the highway carries on to Sudbury, the nickel capital of Canada. There are few trees around Sudbury; the earth is covered by rock. This area is part of the geological region known as the Great Canadian Shield; nearly all of northern Ontario and Quebec are a part of the Shield. There is a lot of mining throughout the whole region, and some forestry, but very little farming.

The next large city on the Trans Canada Highway is Ottawa, the capital of Canada. The Ottawa river is the border between Ontario and Quebec. Visitors will

Toronto is Canada's largest city

A farmhouse in the Quebec countryside

Government of Canada

Government of Canada

see a lot of rich farmland outside Ottawa on the way to Montreal. Montreal is the second largest city in Canada; it is also the second largest French speaking city in the world (Paris is the largest). Quebec City, the oldest city in Canada, is a four-hour drive from Montreal on the Trans Canada Highway.

6 From Quebec City, the highway goes along the St. Lawrence River, then turns south toward New Brunswick. New Brunswick is one of the four Atlantic provinces. New Brunswick is covered by green forests. Just east of Moncton, New Brunswick, the Trans Canada Highway forks in two directions. You can go to Prince Edward Island (P.E.I.) by ferry or carry on to Nova Scotia. Prince Edward Island is the smallest province in Canada; it is known for its beautiful red sand beaches and green countryside.

7 Nova Scotians are never far from water or trees — this small province is almost completely surrounded by the Atlantic Ocean and covered with forests. At Sydney, the northern tip of the province, you can take a ferry to Newfoundland and drive

Potato Fields near Birch Hill, P.E.I. Potatoes are a major crop on the island.

The rugged coast of Port au Port Den, Newfoundland

Bird watchers get up close at the ecological reserve in Cape St. Mary's, Newfoundland

Department of Tourism and Culture, Government of Newfoundland and Labrador

across the island on the Trans Canada Highway. Newfoundland is a rugged, rocky island. Most of the people there come from families who have fished the waters for over a hundred years. Now, however, there are very few fish left and Newfoundlanders are struggling to make a living.

The barren landscape of Baffin Island, Northwest Territories

Government of Canada

8   Although the Trans Canada Highway crosses the southern part of Canada, it does not go to some of the more important cities, for example, Toronto (Canada's largest city), Edmonton, and Halifax. However, there are major roads which connect the highway to these cities.

9   The largest region of Canada, the North, cannot be reached on the Trans Canada Highway. Most travelers go to the North by plane, although there are roads to Yellowknife, Whitehorse and Inuvik. The North is a huge area where very few people live. Much of the ground in the far North is frozen all year around. The North is divided into two Territories — Yukon and the Northwest Territories. The Northwest Territories are soon going to be divided into two separate territories. The new territory (the eastern half of what is now Northwest Territories) will be called Nunavut.

COMPREHENSION AND DISCUSSION QUESTIONS

- 🍃 How do you get from Victoria to Vancouver?
- 🍃 Why do tourists visit Banff and Jasper?
- 🍃 Which provinces make up the Prairies?
- 🍃 What are the Territories?
- 🍃 Is the land good for farming around Sudbury?
- 🍃 Which provinces in Canada have you visited?
- 🍃 Which cities have you visited?
- 🍃 Do you have friends or family who live in other provinces?
- 🍃 Where do they live? How often do you see them?

- Where would you like to visit in Canada? Why?
- What is the farthest north you have ever been in Canada?

LANGUAGE AND CONTACT ACTIVITIES

1. Canada's Industries and Resources

On the chart below, fill in information about the landscape of the five regions. The landscape of the west coast has been done for you.

Region	Province or Territory	Industries & Resources	Landscape
West Coast	British Columbia	Forestry, Fishing, Tourism, Fruit Farms, Cattle Ranches	Pacific Ocean, mountains, forests
The Prairies	Alberta	Oil & Gas; Wheat; Cattle, Tourism	
	Saskatchewan	Wheat, Mining (potash)	
	Manitoba	Wheat, Hydroelectricity	
Central Canada	Ontario	Manufacturing, Mining (nickel, gold, zinc, copper) Fruit, Tourism	
	Quebec	Manufacturing, Hydroelectricity, Tourism, Mining, Dairy Farms	
Atlantic Provinces	New Brunswick	Forestry, Food Processing	
	Nova Scotia	Fishing, Mining, Tourism	
	Prince Edward Island	Potato Farms, Tourism	
	Newfoundland	Fishing, Oil	
The North	Yukon	Fur, Mining, Oil & Gas, Arts & Crafts	
	Northwest Territories		

- Which region do you live in?
- What industries and resources are most common where you live?
- Do you work in one of the industries listed in the chart?

2. Canadian Vacation

Choose a place in Canada that you would like to visit. Find it on a map and answer the following questions:

- What is the name of the place?
- Where is it?
- How far away is it from your home?
- How will you get there?
- Which provinces and/or territories will you travel through or over to get there?
- Is it near a lake, river or ocean? If yes, what is the name of the water?
- What is the land like? Is it near the mountains? the prairies?
- Who will go with you?
- When will you go?
- What will you do when you are there?
- How long will you stay?

WEATHER AND CLIMATE

Canadians like to talk about the weather. The weather can change very quickly. The chinooks of southern Alberta are a good example. Warm, dry winds blow over the Rocky Mountains and can raise the temperature in Calgary from -15°C to +10°C within a few hours.

The climates in Canada's five regions are all different. On a winter day, the temperature in Victoria may be +10 °C while in Whitehorse and Montreal, it may be -30°C. Canadians enjoy long hours of sunlight in the summer; many people play sports or just sit outside until late into the evening. In the winter, people are used to very short days and long nights. In northern towns such as Inuvik, the sun doesn't rise at all in the middle of the winter. The North is called the Land of the Midnight Sun in the summer because people can enjoy up to 24 hours of daylight.

When people first come to Canada, they are often shocked by the weather. They know before they come that Canada has cold winters, but you have to live through a winter before you can really understand why people plug in their cars, wear several layers of clothes, and use a lot of energy to heat their houses.

FOLLOW-UP

- When Canadians talk to strangers, they often talk about the weather. It is the easiest way to start a conversation. What do strangers talk about in your first country?
- In your community, how many ways are there to find out what the weather forecast is for tomorrow?
- Listen to the news on the radio or TV. Find out what the weather forecast is for tomorrow.
- What's the coldest temperature you have ever experienced? The hottest?

3. Where Would You Like to Live?

Ask five people outside your class this question:

If you could live anywhere in Canada, where would that be? Why?

Write down the answers on the chart below. Compare your answers with those of your classmates.

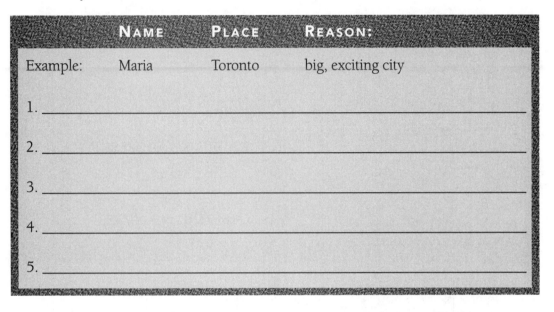

	NAME	PLACE	REASON:
Example:	Maria	Toronto	big, exciting city
1.			
2.			
3.			
4.			
5.			

THE ENVIRONMENT

The environment has become an important issue in Canada and other parts of the world. Many scientists say that if we don't change our way of living, we will destroy the earth. Already many rivers, lakes and oceans are polluted; the air is not clean, and forests and animals are dying. Some people think it is almost too late to save the environment, but others are sure that if we all start to take care of the environment, we can make a difference.

Many cities have started recycling programs where bottles, cans, newspaper, regular paper, cardboard, plastic and metal are collected and processed for reuse. Individuals and companies have started to use less energy, less water and fewer polluting chemicals. Many people think that the only way to save the environment is to follow the three Rs: Reduce, Reuse and Recycle.

FOLLOW-UP

- What environmental problems do you think affect Canada the most?

- What environmental problems affect you personally?

- What are some different ways to reduce, reuse and recycle?

- Do you think that one person can make a difference to the environment?

4. Writing to the Tourist Bureau

Write a letter to the Tourist Bureau closest to the place you want to visit. Ask them to send you information about the place.

Your letter should have all of these parts: your address, date, tourist bureau address, greeting, message, closing, signature. For example:

apartment number, street address city, province postal code	YOUR ADDRESS
month, day, year	DATE
tourist bureau name street address city, province postal code	RECEIVER'S ADDRESS
Dear Sir or Madam: I would like some information on Peggy's Cove. Could you please send me any pamphlets containing information on the area around Peggy's Cove? I am interested in campsites nearby, points of historical interest, and hiking trails in the area. Thank you for your consideration.	GREETING MESSAGE
Sincerely,	CLOSING
Signature	SIGNATURE

GLOSSARY OF TERMS

NOUNS

border: invisible line separating two countries or provinces

climate: a combination of temperature, precipitation (rain or snow), wind, etc.

currency: money

democracy: a government which is elected by the people, and which can be changed by the people

ferry: a boat which takes cars and/or people across water

food processing: preparing frozen or canned foods

foothills: large hills close to mountains

forecast: weather prediction

forestry: the business of cutting trees and turning them into lumber and paper

individual: one person

manufacturing: making things in factories, e.g., cars

mining: taking minerals such as gold or iron from the earth

pamphlet: a booklet or brochure

population: total number of people in a place

prairie: flat, dry land

rodeo: a competition where cowboys ride wild horses, rope cattle, and perform in other events

tourism: hotels, restaurants, sightseeing tours, travel

VERBS

to connect: join

ADJECTIVES

polluted: dirty or spoiled, unfit for use

TEST YOURSELF

What does Canada look like?

MULTIPLE CHOICE

Circle the best answer.

1. Canada is the _____ country in the world.
   A) largest   B) second largest
   C) third largest   D) fourth largest

2. Canada has _____ official language(s).
   A) one   B) two
   C) three   D) more than three

3. Canada has _____.
   A) eight provinces   B) ten provinces
   C) four territories   D) one territory

4. Fredericton is the capital of _____.
   A) Nova Scotia   B) Prince Edward Island
   C) New Brunswick   D) Newfoundland

5. The largest city in Canada is _____.
   A) Toronto   B) Ottawa
   C) Montreal   D) Vancouver

6. The capital of Canada is _____.
   A) Toronto   B) Ottawa
   C) Montreal   D) Vancouver

7. Canada is bordered by all but the _____ ocean.
   A) Arctic   B) Pacific
   C) Atlantic   D) Indian

8. Which of the following is a major industry in British Columbia?
   A) Oil & Gas   B) Mining
   C) Fishing   D) Manufacturing

9. Which of the following is a major industry in Newfoundland?
   A) Oil & Gas   B) Manufacturing
   C) Farming   D) Forestry

TRUE/FALSE

Circle T if the statement is true. Circle F if it is false.

1. Canada is made up of twelve provinces. T / F

2. The capital city of Canada is Ontario. T / F

3. The capital of British Columbia is Vancouver. T / F

4. The capital of Ontario is Montreal. T / F

5. Vancouver is the third largest city in Canada. T / F

6. The population of Canada is approximately 27 million. T / F

7. Canada is surrounded by two oceans. T / F

8. Most Canadians live in the southern part of Canada. T / F

9. One of the main industries of Saskatchewan is fishing. T / F

10. One of the main industries of Alberta is oil & gas. T / F

11. Mining is an important industry in Ontario. T / F

FILL IN THE BLANKS

In the blank, write the word(s) needed to make the sentence complete.

1. The population of Canada is approximately _____ million.

2. _____ is the capital of Yukon.

3. The country to the south of Canada is _____.

4. _____ is the capital city of Saskatchewan.

5. St. John's is the capital city of _____.

6. The largest city in Canada is _____.

7. The official languages of Canada are _____ and _____.

8. Canada is made up of _____ provinces and _____ territories.

9. The capital city of British Columbia is _____.

10. Canada is surrounded by the _____, _____, and _____ oceans.

MATCHING
Match each capital city with the province/territory it belongs to.

A. British Columbia   ___ Yellowknife

B. Alberta   ___ Fredericton

C. Saskatchewan   ___ Edmonton

D. Manitoba   ___ Charlottetown

E. Ontario   ___ Whitehorse

F. Quebec   ___ Toronto

G. New Brunswick   ___ Regina

H. Nova Scotia   ___ Winnipeg

I. Prince Edward Island   ___ Victoria

J. Newfoundland   ___ Halifax

K. Northwest Territories   ___ Quebec City

L. Yukon   ___ St. John's

SHORT ANSWER
Answer the following questions.

1. Which oceans surround Canada?

_____

2. What was the last province to join Confederation?

_____

3. List the Great Lakes.

_____

4. Name the prairie provinces.

_____

5. What is a chinook?

_____

6. What will be the name of the new territory in the north?

_____

7. Canadians strongly believe in saving the environment.
   What do the three Rs stand for?

_____

8. What are the four Atlantic provinces?

_____

9. What are three main industries of the prairie provinces?

_____

10. What are three main industries of the Atlantic provinces?

_____

Chapter 2   Canada's First Peoples

MATERIALS REQUIRED Maps of Canada and the world, *The Canadian Encyclopedia*, and information and pictures related to Native peoples in your area.

SKILLS EMPHASIZED Map-reading skills, letter writing, reading a timeline, discussing, planning, listing ideas, reading for information, explaining, expressing opinions.

PRE-READING I

Canada is made up of many different people.

PEOPLE	ARRIVAL	REASON FOR COMING TO CANADA
Indians (First Nations)	30 000 years ago	to hunt, farm and fish
Inuit	5 000 years ago	to hunt and fish
English	1497	to fish
French	1534	to hunt, farm, trade furs
Chinese	about 1870	to build the railroad
Other Europeans	1885–1910	to farm
People from elsewhere	present	freedom to start a new life

🐦 Have you ever heard of Indian, Inuit and Métis people?

🐦 Who were the first people to come to Canada?

🐦 How much longer have the Inuit been in Canada than the English?

🐦 For what reasons do most people come to Canada now?

🐦 When did you come to Canada? Why did you come to Canada?

🐦 If you had to do it over, would you still come to Canada?

Here is a timeline. Above the timeline are dates. Below the timeline are events. Fill in the information from the chart on page 22.

30 000 years ago		5000 years ago	1497	1534		1885-1913		now	

Indians   My arrival in Canada

READING I: INDIANS, INUIT AND MÉTIS

The first people to come to Canada were the Indians. Scientists think that they came from Asia across the Bering Strait about 30 000 years ago. When they arrived in North America they traveled south and east. After several hundred years there were many groups of Native people who had different cultures and languages. There are more than 50 Indian languages in Canada. Today, North American Indians are often called First Nations Peoples.

2   The Indian people who lived by the coasts hunted and fished. Prairie Indians moved from place to place, hunting the buffalo. They ate buffalo meat and used buffalo hides to make clothing and teepees. Some Native people who lived in central and eastern Canada were farmers. They grew corn and vegetables.

A totem pole in Alert Bay, Vancouver Island

Provincial Archives of Alberta

Huge herds of buffalo roamed the prairies before the arrival of the Europeans

Provincial Archives of Alberta

Potlatches were celebrations at which groups of West Coast Indians feasted and exchanged gifts

British Columbia Archives and Records Service

Indian Potlatch Duncan BC.

3   The Inuit (also called Eskimo), came to Canada from Asia about 5000 years ago. They moved across the north from Alaska to Greenland, and learned to live in a land of ice and snow. They lived by hunting seals, whales, caribou, and polar bears. Many lived in ice houses called *igloos*. Today many Inuit still hunt. Most live in small towns in northern Canada.

4   In the 1500s, people from Europe started to come to Canada to live. Some Native people showed them how to survive. They helped them with food and shelter. They guided explorers to new lands and helped to establish the fur trade. Some Native people married Europeans. Their children were called Métis. The

Inuit mother and child from Iqaluit, Northwest Territories

Government of Canada

Métis people developed their own culture and customs. The Indians, the Inuit, and the Métis are citizens of Canada today.

COMPREHENSION AND DISCUSSION QUESTIONS

1. When did the Indian people come to Canada?
2. When did the Inuit come to Canada?
3. How did the Indian people survive?
4. Where do the Inuit live today?
5. What did you know about Canada's Native people before you came to Canada?
6. What do you know about the Native people in your community?
7. Are there any whales, seals, caribou or bears in the country you came from? What animals live in the wild there?

LANGUAGE AND CONTACT ACTIVITIES

1. Hunting and Fishing

Use your telephone directory to find the government departments responsible for hunting and fishing licences. Answer the questions on the following page.

- How much does a hunting licence cost?
- How much does a fishing licence cost?
- Where can you hunt?
- Where can you fish?
- Are there places where hunting and fishing are not allowed?
- What animals can be hunted?

Some people see hunting as a sport. That is, they hunt for fun. Other people only hunt for food. Do you think hunting should be allowed as a sport?

2. Map Reading: The World

In pairs, look at a map of the world. Locate Asia, North America, Canada, Alaska, and the Bering Strait. Mark the route the Native people took to come to Canada. How do you think the Native people came to Canada?

3. Map Reading: Canada

Inuit people still live in northern Canada. On a map of Canada, locate the Inuit communities of Inuvik, Iqaluit (Frobisher Bay), Arviat (Eskimo Point), Rankin Inlet, and Tuktoyaktuk. How far are each of these places from where you live? Which place is the closest? Which is the farthest?

PRE-READING II

- What do you think happened when the Europeans first met the Native people in Canada?
- Have you heard of smallpox, measles, tuberculosis? Were these diseases ever a problem in the country you came from?
- Do you know what an Indian reserve is?

READING II: NATIVE VALUES

1 When the Europeans came to Canada, the life of the Native people changed forever. Europeans brought serious diseases such as smallpox, measles, and tuberculosis. Tens of thousands of Native people died.

2 When the Europeans started colonies in the Atlantic provinces and central Canada, farming became important. Indians were forced off their lands and onto small reserves (land for Native use only). For many years, Native people have

been unhappy with the way the Europeans treated them. They want agreements that will give them the land that they feel belongs to them.

Losing people to disease and losing land to the Europeans were not the *3* only problems faced by Native people. Native people's values are very different from European values. The ideas of cooperation, sharing, and respect for the land are important to the Native peoples. Europeans value individual achievement and private ownership.

Today, Native people face many serious social problems including discrimination, poor education, alcoholism, and high unemployment. There are some *4* people who have a stereotyped idea about Native people, for example, they think that all Native people receive a living allowance from the government. In fact, many Native people do not receive a living allowance or any other government assistance. Native people in cities and on reserves are trying to get greater control over their lives; they want to solve their problems and many would like to have self-government.

COMPREHENSION AND DISCUSSION QUESTIONS:

1. When the Europeans first came to Canada, they tried to force the Native people to adopt European culture. What were the effects?
2. Which values of the Native peoples and which values of the Europeans caused conflicts? Why?
3. Do you think that a person must give up his/her own culture in order to become a Canadian?
4. Native people experience a lot of discrimination. Why do you think this is? Have you experienced any discrimination as an immigrant? What can we do to stop discrimination?
5. How are Native and European values different?
6. Which do you think the Canadian government values more — individual rights or society's rights? Which do you think is more important?

LANGUAGE AND CONTACT ACTIVITIES

1. Invite a Guest Speaker to Class

Write a letter to your local Native Friendship Centre or Native Community Centre to invite a guest speaker to your class to talk about Native issues. Make up a list of questions to ask the guest speaker. A list has been started for you.

- What languages do you speak?
- Are there many Native people in _____? (name of city/town)
- What does the Native Friendship Centre do?

2. Plan a Field Trip to Your Local Museum

As a group, make up a list of questions to ask the museum. Some questions you might ask are:

- Does the museum have a Native people's display?
- When is the museum open?
- How much does it cost?

Choose one student to phone the museum, find out the answers to the questions, arrange a date for the class to visit the museum and report back to the rest of the class.

3. Newspaper Stories

Look through your local newspaper for one week. Find one article about Native people. Bring the article to class. In pairs, tell your partner about the article by answering the following questions:

- Who is the article about?
- What happened?
- Where did it happen?
- When did it happen?

4. Aboriginal Words

The word *Canada* comes from the aboriginal word *kanata* meaning *village*. Many place names in Canada come from aboriginal languages, for example, *Saskatchewan* and *Ottawa*. *Saskatchewan* comes from a Cree word meaning *swiftly flowing river*. *Ottawa* comes from the name of a tribe; it means *to trade*. Name three places that come from aboriginal words, and then find their meanings in the *Canadian Encyclopedia*.

THE NATIVE LAND CLAIMS ISSUE

Once Europeans gained control of what is now Canada, they began to make land agreements with the Native people. That is, they offered to let the Native people keep small areas of land that would be for Native use only (reserves). Some Native groups received reserve land; others did not. Recently, several Native groups have argued that they should be given back the land that was taken away from them. The federal, provincial, and territorial governments are meeting with some Native groups. Some Native bands have been successful; the government has given them more land and/or money. Other Native bands are still fighting for their land, for example, the Lubicon Indians in northern Alberta.

FOLLOW-UP

All of North America once belonged to the Native people. Do you think it is fair that the land was taken away from them? Do you think that the land that was taken away should be given back?

Look up the *Lubicon Indians* in *The Canadian Encyclopedia*. Try to answer the following questions:

- Who are the Lubicons?
- Where do they live?
- When did they start to argue about land with the government?
- What happened?

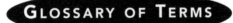

GLOSSARY OF TERMS

NOUNS

achievement: success
alcoholism: addiction to alcohol
buffalo: a large animal that lived on the Prairies
colonies: villages set up by Europeans in places outside Europe
conflict: disagreement or argument
cooperation: working together
culture: the beliefs, values, and lifestyle of a group of people

discrimination: prejudging on the basis of sex, skin colour, religion, etc.; prejudice

disease: sickness, illness, e.g., smallpox, flu, malaria, cholera, tuberculosis

hide: the skin of an animal

individual: one person

Inuit: aboriginal people who live in the north, also called Eskimo

Native people: aboriginal people, Indians, First Nations people

private ownership: things belong to individuals, not to the community

reserve: land owned by Native people

respect: appreciation, good treatment

teepee: a tent made of hides and wooden poles

values: what people believe in

Canada's First Peoples

MULTIPLE CHOICE

Circle the best answer.

1. Who were the first people to come to Canada?
   A) the English
   B) the French
   C) the Indians
   D) the Americans

2. How many Indian languages are there in Canada today?
   A) less than 10
   B) 10-20
   C) 25-50
   D) more than 50

3. People whose parents (or ancestors) are both Native and European are called:
   A) Inuit
   B) Métis
   C) Inuvik
   D) Mohawk

4. Indians came to Canada approximately _____ years ago.
   A) 50 000
   B) 30 000
   C) 5000
   D) 3000

5. An area of land that is set aside for use by Native people only is called:
   A) a reserve
   B) Indiana
   C) an Indian band
   D) a territory

TRUE/FALSE

Circle T if the statement is true. Circle F if it is false.

1. Europeans brought many diseases to the aboriginal peoples   T / F

2. The English were the first to come to Canada.   T / F

3. All Native people speak the same language.   T / F

4. The Indian people helped the Europeans to survive.   T / F

5. Métis are people whose parents are both
   Native and European.   T / F

FILL IN THE BLANKS

In the blank, write the word(s) needed to make the sentence complete.

1. The Inuit lived in ice houses called _____.

2. The Indian people came to Canada approximately _____ years ago.

3. The Inuit came to Canada approximately _____ years ago.

4. The English first arrived in Canada in _____.

5. The French first settled in Canada in _____.

6. The Indian people living on the coasts survived by _____ and _____.

7. The Indian people living on the prairies survived by _____.

8. The Indian people living in central Canada survived by _____.

9. The Indian people were forced off their land and onto _____.

SHORT ANSWER

Answer the following questions.

1. How do scientists think Indian people came to Canada?

_____

2. What happened to the Indian people when Europeans first came to Canada?

_____

3. What is a reserve?

_____

4. List two values of Native people.

_____

5. List three problems that Native people face today.

_____

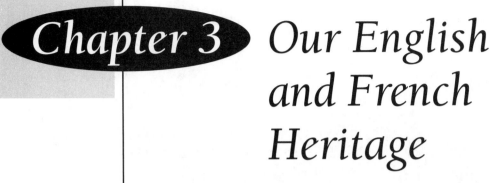

Chapter 3 Our English and French Heritage

MATERIALS REQUIRED Map of North America, pictures and other resources about early French and English settlers, *The Canadian Encyclopedia*.

SKILLS EMPHASIZED Reading comprehension, discussion, expressing an opinion, comparing, listing, evaluating, describing, organizing information, predicting, listening, giving instructions.

PRE-READING I

- On a map of Canada, find Newfoundland, Quebec City, and the Saint Lawrence River.

- Are there very many French speakers in your community? Do you have a French TV station? Radio station? Are there many French immersion schools in your community?

READING I: THE ENGLISH AND FRENCH COME TO CANADA

In 1497 Giovanni Caboto (also known as John Cabot) sailed from England to Newfoundland. He claimed the land for the King of England. The English were glad that Caboto found Canada because the fishing was very good. Every summer, many ships would sail to Newfoundland to fish off the Grand Banks and then would return to England for the winter.

1

In the early 1500s the French came to Canada. They were the first permanent settlers from Europe. They set up fur trading posts in Acadia (parts of Nova Scotia,

2

Fur traders on the Athabasca river

Provincial Archives of Alberta

New Brunswick and Prince Edward Island) and along the St. Lawrence River. The first Canadian city, Quebec City, was founded by Samuel de Champlain on the site of an older Indian village called Stadacona. The French lived by hunting, farming and fur trading with the Indians (First Nations people). The First Nations people brought pelts of beaver and other animals to the French, who traded blankets and trinkets in return. The French then sold the pelts in Europe for a lot of money.

3   The English began to settle in Canada too. There were many struggles between the French and the English for control of Canada. In 1763, at the end of the Seven Years' War (between England and France), France was forced to give all its land in North America to England. The Canadian colonies now had an English king, but the majority of the people who lived there were French.

4   Although the colonies in what is now Quebec came under British control, the Quebec Act of 1774 gave the people in that region some basic rights (freedom of religion and French civil law).

5   The British traveled to the West, where they set up fur trading posts and settlements. Today, English is spoken by the majority of people in Canada. The Canadian system of government is based on the British system.

6   Today, about 80 percent of the people living in Quebec speak French as a first language. French speakers are found in every part of Canada. There are French newspapers, radio and TV stations across the country.

COMPREHENSION AND DISCUSSION QUESTIONS

1. Why did the English come to Newfoundland every summer?
2. Who were the first European settlers in Canada?
3. What was the first city in Canada?
4. Which province has the most French speaking people?
5. What did the English and French trade with the First Nations people?
6. Do you speak French?

LANGUAGE AND CONTACT ACTIVITIES

1. Finding Two Sides to an Issue

Fur has always been important in Canada's history. Today there are people called animal rights activists who are against the killing of animals for any reason. They try to stop people from eating meat and wearing clothes made of animal hides. They also try to stop researchers from using animals in their experiments. In pairs, make a list of the advantages and disadvantages of using animals for food, clothing, and research:

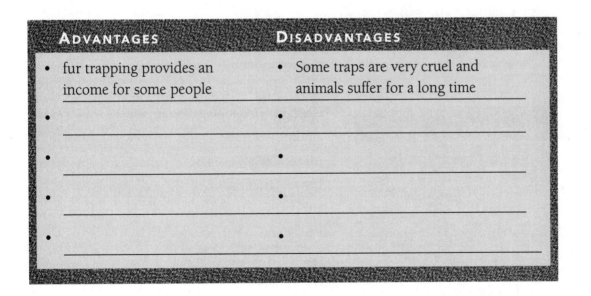

ADVANTAGES	DISADVANTAGES
• fur trapping provides an income for some people	• Some traps are very cruel and animals suffer for a long time
•	•
•	•
•	•
•	•

Share your list with the class.

2. Debate

Divide the class into two teams. One team must argue for the benefits of using animals and the other team must argue for animal rights. Take ten minutes to plan your argument. Choose a speaker for each group. Flip a coin to decide who goes first. Each speaker talks for two minutes. Then, for ten minutes, the teams help the speaker find arguments against what the other team has said. Each team has four minutes to argue their points. The teacher decides which team is most convincing.

3. History of Your Community

Find out about the history of your community by researching the following questions. Have someone in your class phone the local librarian and ask these questions.

- How did your town or city get its name?
- Who were the first European settlers in your area?
- When did the first settlers come?
- When did your community become a city?
- What is the population of your city?
- Was your city ever a trading post?
- Was there a native village on the site of your community?
- Is there a museum or historical monument in your city that tells about our French and English history?

If there is a museum or historical monument in your city, plan a trip to see it.

4. Famous Historical Figures

Choose one of the following names and, using *The Canadian Encyclopedia*, find out why the person you have chosen is important in Canadian history:

Captain James Cook
Captain George Vancouver
Anthony Henday
Alexander Mackenzie
David Thompson
Simon Fraser
Paul Kane
Radisson & Groseilliers
Henry Kelsey
Sieur de la Verendrye
Jean Talon
Laura Secord
Father Lacombe
Susanna Moodie

THE ST. LAWRENCE RIVER

Native guides first led Jacques Cartier, a French explorer, to the St. Lawrence River in 1535. In 1608, Samuel de Champlain, another French explorer, set up a permanent settlement on the St. Lawrence at what is now Quebec City. Throughout the years the St. Lawrence River has been important for trade and industry. The St. Lawrence Seaway was completed in 1959 as a joint effort of the governments of Canada and the USA. It is a series of locks and canals which connects the Great Lakes to the river. The Seaway lets ships travel approximately 3800 kilometres into the centre of North America.

THE HUDSON'S BAY COMPANY

In 1670, the English King gave The Hudson's Bay Company, a British fur trading firm, control over large parts of Ontario, Quebec, Manitoba, Saskatchewan, Alberta and the N.W.T. The Hudson's Bay Company set up nearly one hundred trading posts, many of which are now Canadian cities. The land owned by the Hudson's Bay was sold to Canada in 1870. The Bay department stores that are in most Canadian cities are owned by the Hudson's Bay Company.

Trading at a Hudson's Bay Company trading post

Provincial Archives of Alberta

PRE-READING II

- Find the Atlantic provinces on a map of North America.
- Find Louisiana in the U.S.A.
- Calculate how many kilometres it is from Halifax, Nova Scotia, to New Orleans, Louisiana.
- How long do you think it would take a person to walk that distance?

READING II: THE ACADIANS

1   The French settlers who came to Nova Scotia in the 1600s were called *Acadians*. In the 1700s Britain and France were at war. Although England had control over Nova Scotia after 1713, the English settlers were very worried about the large number of French Acadian farmers in the area. The Acadians claimed to be neutral; that is, they promised not to fight the British, or to help France, but the British didn't trust them.

2   In 1755 the British government told the Acadians that they must swear allegiance to the English King or be deported from Nova Scotia. The Acadians did not want to swear allegiance because they were afraid they would have to fight their own people, the French. They wanted to be left alone to farm.

3   The English began to force the Acadians out of the area. Nearly 15 000 Acadians were deported. Many families were split up and people had no choice of where they could go. Some Acadians escaped to Quebec and returned to Nova Scotia and New Brunswick when the English and French stopped fighting. Many Acadians moved to Louisiana where they set up new communities. Today there are still descendants of the Acadians in Louisiana; they are called *Cajuns*.

COMPREHENSION AND DISCUSSION QUESTIONS:

1. Why did the English force the Acadians to leave?
2. Where did the Acadians go?
3. What are the Acadians who moved to Louisiana called today?
4. Acadians became refugees. Where are there refugees today?

LANGUAGE AND CONTACT ACTIVITIES:

1. Write a Story

Write a short story about an Acadian family deported to Louisiana. Describe the farm where they lived, how the English forced them out and the long journey to Louisiana. Some information has been provided for you.

ACADIAN DEPORTATION — INFORMATION

Who: Jacques and Claudette Hebert and their children, François, Isabelle, Luc, Michelle.

When: Dinner time, June 21, 1755

Where: The Hebert farmhouse in Acadia.

What happened: English soldiers came through the door holding guns. They ordered the Heberts to leave. The Heberts had ten minutes to get their things together. The Heberts walked to Louisiana.

Why: The English were afraid of the Acadians.

Write your story using complete sentences. Give your story a title. Exchange your story with someone else. Read your partner's story. Correct any errors you find.

CANADA: ONE COUNTRY OR MANY?

Although Canada has been an independent country since 1867, there have always been struggles between different groups. In Quebec, for example, there have always been French people who are unhappy with English dominance. They think that separation from the rest of Canada is the only way to maintain their French identity. In the 1960s the Parti Quebecois (PQ), a provincial political party committed to independence, was formed. In 1976, the PQ became the provincial government of Quebec. In 1980, the people of Quebec voted to decide whether they wanted to separate from Canada. Although the majority decided not to separate, there are still many Quebeckers today who want Quebec to be a separate country. Recently a federal political party was formed, the Bloc Quebecois. They are committed to separating from the rest of Canada.

People from Quebec are not the only ones who want more independence. The First Nations people would like to have more control over their lives. Also, some people in western Canada feel that the federal government has too much control. Canada is a unique country because it is so big and yet has a small population made up of many different groups of people. There may always be struggles; national unity will always be difficult to achieve.

FOLLOW-UP

Divide into groups of four. Discuss the following questions:

Do you think Quebec *should* separate from the rest of Canada? Explain your answer.

Do you think Quebec *will* separate from the rest of Canada? Explain.

If Quebec separates,

- will there be violence?
- what will happen to the English people living in Quebec?
- what will happen to First Nations people living in Quebec?
- what will happen to other non-French speaking groups?

2. Giving Directions

A friend of yours is visiting from the country you came from. She wants to go shopping, but you can't go with her because you have to go to school. You bring her to your ESL class to visit for a few minutes, and then you give her directions to the closest Bay store. Write out the directions from your school to the Bay. Compare your set of directions with other students' directions. Are they the same? Is anyone's friend going to get lost?

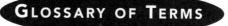

GLOSSARY OF TERMS

NOUNS

descendent: opposite of ancestor

dominance: powerful influence

guide: someone who shows the way

identity: what a person or thing is

national unity: one identity; shared values within a country

pelt: animal hide; fur

separation: splitting up

settlers: people who come to live in a new land

struggles: conflicts

trading post: a place where people exchanged goods

VERBS

to achieve: to succeed; to get

to deport: to send away

to escape: to get away

to force: to make someone do something against his/her will

to settle: to establish a new home

to swear allegiance: to promise loyalty

ADJECTIVES

independent: self-governing

neutral: neither for nor against

permanent: lasting; not temporary

Test Yourself

Our English and French Heritage

MULTIPLE CHOICE

Circle the best answer.

1. Newfoundland was claimed for the King of England in 1497 by:
   A) Sir Wilfrid Laurier
   B) Samuel de Champlain
   C) Pierre Trudeau
   D) Giovanni Caboto

2. The first Canadian city was _____.
   A) Ottawa
   B) Montreal
   C) Toronto
   D) Quebec City

3. Quebec City was built by _____.
   A) Sir Wilfrid Laurier
   B) Samuel de Champlain
   C) Jacques Cartier
   D) Giovanni Caboto

4. The French lived by doing all of the following except _____.
   A) hunting
   B) fishing
   C) trading with the Indians
   D) mining

5. Many Acadians moved to _____ after being deported.
   A) Louisiana
   B) Acadia
   C) New Brunswick
   D) British Columbia

6. What is the name of the federal party devoted to the separation of Quebec?
   A) Parti Quebecois
   B) Reform Party
   C) Bloc Quebecois
   D) Conservative Party

TRUE/FALSE

Circle T if the statement is true. Circle F if it is false.

1. Newfoundland was claimed for the King of England in 1497 by Samuel de Champlain.　　　　T / F

2. The first Canadian city was Montreal.　　　　T / F

3. Quebec City was founded by Wilfrid Laurier.　　　　T / F

4. Many Acadians moved to Yukon after being deported from Acadia.　　　　T / F

5. The French settlers who came to Nova Scotia in the
   1600s were called Acadians.   T / F

FILL IN THE BLANKS
In the blank, write the word(s) needed to make the sentence complete.

1. The Seven Years' War was a war between _____ and

   _____.

2. The _____ Act of 1774 provided the French people with

   some basic rights.

3. The French settlers who came to Nova Scotia in the 1600s were called

   _____.

4. Some people in Quebec think that the only way to maintain their French

   identity is to _____.

5. Quebec's first vote on separation occurred in _____.

SHORT ANSWER
Answer the following questions.

1. What percentage of people living in Quebec speak French as their first
   language?

   _____

2. Which Atlantic provinces make up Acadia?

   _____

3. Where did most Acadians move to after being deported from Acadia?

   _____

4. What provincial political party was formed in Quebec in the 1960s?

   _____

5. What federal political party was recently formed that is committed
   to the separation of Quebec from Canada?

   _____

Chapter 4 Confederation

MATERIALS REQUIRED Copies of the portion of your telephone directory that lists federal, provincial and municipal services; a calendar; newspapers; a tape recording of "O Canada!"

SKILLS EMPHASIZED Reading comprehension, discussion, comparing and contrasting; locating information; problem solving; finding the main idea.

PRE-READING I

- What holidays do Canadians celebrate?
- What did you do on Canada Day (July 1)?
- How does your community celebrate Canada Day?
- Why do we celebrate Canada Day?
- What holidays did you celebrate in your first country?

READING I: CANADA BECOMES A COUNTRY

1 Canada became a country on July 1, 1867. The provinces of Quebec, Ontario, New Brunswick and Nova Scotia joined to become a single country. The other provinces and territories joined Canada after 1867. The last to join was Newfoundland in 1949. The joining of provinces to make a new country is called Confederation. Sir John A. Macdonald was the first Prime Minister of Canada. His picture is on the ten dollar bill. We celebrate Confederation with a holiday every year on July 1, Canada Day.

Sir John A. Macdonald was the first prime minister of Canada

National Archives of Canada

PROVINCES/TERRITORIES	TIME OF ENTRY TO CONFEDERATION
Ontario, Quebec, Nova Scotia, New Brunswick	1867
Manitoba; Northwest Territories	1870
British Columbia	1871
Prince Edward island	1873
Yukon	1898
Alberta, Saskatchewan	1905
Newfoundland	1949

COMPREHENSION AND DISCUSSION QUESTIONS

1. When did your province join Confederation?
2. What was the last province to join?
3. Who was the first prime minister of Canada?
4. Who is the prime minister of Canada today?

LANGUAGE AND CONTACT ACTIVITIES

1. National Holidays

In Canada there are several national holidays as well as provincial and municipal holidays. On these days, most government offices, banks and schools are closed. Listed below are the national holidays. Find out what dates they are on for this year and the purpose of each holiday. You can use a calendar to get the dates; ask a friend or neighbour what is celebrated on these days if you are not sure.

HOLIDAY	DATE	PURPOSE
Canada Day	July 1	To celebrate Canada's birthday
Christmas		
Thanksgiving		
Good Friday		
Remembrance Day		
New Year's Day		
Victoria Day		
Labour Day		
Boxing Day		
Easter		

2. Other Holidays

People celebrate other holidays in Canada. Compare the national days of all the countries represented in your class. Do your classmates celebrate these days now that they live in Canada? How are these national days celebrated?

There are also special days in Canada which are not official holidays. These include Valentine's Day, St. Patrick's Day, Halloween, Mother's Day, Father's Day, birthdays, and wedding anniversaries. People often send each other cards on these days.

Answer the following questions.

- ❧ When is Valentine's Day?
- ❧ When is St. Patrick's Day?
- ❧ When is Halloween?
- ❧ When is Mother's Day?

Louis Riel was a Métis activist in
the late 1800s

LOUIS RIEL

In 1870, the people in what is now Manitoba were deciding whether or not to join Canada. At that time, the majority of people in Manitoba were Native or Métis. Many Native people and Métis did not want Manitoba to join Confederation. They did not believe that Canada would be a good place for them. They wanted a separate country for themselves. Louis Riel, a Métis, led a rebellion to stop Manitoba from joining Canada. There was a struggle between the Native people and the European settlers. Riel was defeated and Manitoba joined Confederation. Although he was later hanged for treason, many Canadians think Riel was a hero who fought for aboriginal rights.

🍂 When is Father's Day?

🍂 How do Canadians celebrate these special days?

🍂 When is your birthday? How do you celebrate your birthday?

🍂 Are you married? If you are, do you celebrate your wedding anniversary?

3. Let's Sing!

Canadians sing the national anthem (see lyrics to O Canada! at the side) at hockey games, rodeos, baseball games and other sporting events. They also sing it at Citizenship ceremonies and on Canada Day. As a class, sing O Canada!

What is the national anthem of your first country? When do people sing it? What does each line mean?

THE CANADIAN NATIONAL ANTHEM: O CANADA!

O Canada!
Our home and native land!
True patriot love in all thy sons command.
With glowing hearts we see thee rise,
The true North strong and free.
From far and wide, O Canada
we stand on guard for thee.
God keep our land glorious and free.
O Canada, we stand on guard for thee.
O Canada, we stand on guard for thee.

PRE-READING II

Here are some of the responsibilities of each level of government in Canada.

RESPONSIBILITIES OF THE THREE LEVELS OF GOVERNMENT		
Federal Responsibilities	**Provincial Responsibilities**	**Municipal Responsibilities**
citizenship	health care	garbage collection
defence	education	recycling
post office	licences	water
unemployment insurance	highways	fire protection
foreign policy		streets
money		city police
Canada Pension		
RCMP		

Canada has three levels of government. The federal government makes laws for the whole country. The provincial and territorial governments make laws that apply in their provinces or territories only. The municipal governments make laws that apply only in their cities or towns. Each level of government has different responsibilities.

🍃 What are the three levels of government in Canada?

🍃 Does your first country have different levels of government?

🍃 Who is responsible for building roads in your country?

🍃 Is there a law in your country that says what the government is responsible for?

🍃 Have you heard of the Constitution in Canada? What do you know about it?

🍃 What government services have you used in the last month?

READING II: THE CONSTITUTION

1 When Canada became a country, the British government passed a law called the British North America Act. This Act was Canada's Constitution, or most important law. It outlined the responsibilities of the Canadian federal government and the provincial governments. For example, the federal government is in charge of printing money. No province is allowed to have its own currency. The provincial governments are responsible for education. Each province has its own educational system.

Her Majesty Queen Elizabeth II signs the Constitution Act 1982 as Prime Minister Pierre Elliott Trudeau looks on

Robert Cooper/National Archives of Canada/PA-140705

The Constitution was kept in England and could not be changed without approval of the British government. In 1982, Prime Minister Pierre Trudeau brought the Constitution back to Canada. The Constitution was changed so that Canada had full control over it. Also, the Canadian Charter of Rights and Freedoms was made a part of the Constitution. The Charter outlines the rights of Canadian citizens (for example, the right to vote). The Constitution is now called The Constitution Act, 1982.

COMPREHENSION AND DISCUSSION QUESTIONS

1. What is a constitution?
2. What was the name of the first constitution of Canada? Where was it kept?
3. Why was the constitution brought back to Canada in 1982?
4. What is the name of the new constitution?

LANGUAGE AND CONTACT ACTIVITIES

1. Locating Government Services in the Phone Book

Working in pairs, use the telephone book to find the numbers for the following services:

✺ police

✺ fire department

✺ citizenship offices

✺ passport office

✺ immigration office

✺ family and social services

✺ tourist bureau

Which level of government is responsible for each of these services?

2. Problem Solving

Which level of government would you call when

✺ there is a mistake on your water bill

✺ you want to get a licence for your dog

✺ you want to get a driver's licence

✺ you want to know how to bring a relative to Canada

✺ you want to get a Canadian passport

✺ there is a pothole on your street

✺ you see someone breaking into your neighbour's house

✺ a landlord will not rent an apartment to people from your country

St. Jean Baptiste day, June 24, also called Fête National, is a holiday at which French Canadians celebrate their heritage

Government of Canada

3. Writing a Constitution

Working in small groups, write a constitution for your class. Outline the responsibilities of the teacher, the students and anyone else who comes to your class. Compare your group's constitution with those of others in the class.

4. Guess the Story

Cut out some newspaper headlines that have to do with government and bring them to class. In small groups ask your classmates to guess from the title what the story was about.

CANADIAN UNITY

In 1982, the Constitution was brought back to Canada. One province, Quebec, decided not to sign it. Over the years, the Conservative government tried to get Quebec to sign the Constitution. There were several meetings of all the premiers and Native leaders. The premier of Quebec wanted Quebec to be recognized in the Constitution as a distinct society. In other words, the people of Quebec wanted their language and cultural differences to be recognized by law.

In Charlottetown, an accord with proposed changes to the constitution was drawn up. A referendum, or vote, was carried out in the fall of 1992. All Canadians over the age of 18 were asked to vote whether or not they wanted the proposed changes to the Constitution to be made. The majority of Canadians voted no. Many people said that they voted no because they were angry with the politicians, not because of the issues. Some Native people were very upset, because the changes to the Constitution would have given them more rights to self-government. Many people in Quebec were upset because they thought that the rest of Canada did not want to recognize their unique identity. Today this is still an unresolved issue.

FOLLOW-UP

- Do you think that Quebec will ever sign the constitution?
- Do you think that certain groups in Canada should be given special rights? Why or why not?

GLOSSARY OF TERMS

NOUNS

approval: permission

hero: a champion, an inspirational person

majority: over 50 percent

politician: a person whose business is politics; a person who is interested in affecting how people are governed

rebellion: revolt; uprising

responsibility: duty

treason: betrayal of country; disloyalty

VERBS

to celebrate: to mark a special event

to hang: to kill someone by putting a rope around the neck (*note*: past tense is "hanged")

to struggle: to fight

ADJECTIVES

distinct: different; unique

former: previous

glorious: wonderful

patriot: love of country

TEST YOURSELF

Confederation

MULTIPLE CHOICE

Circle the best answer.

1. Which was the last province to join Confederation?
   - A) Alberta
   - B) Saskatchewan
   - C) Newfoundland
   - D) Nova Scotia

2. Which province below did not join Confederation until after 1867?
   - A) Ontario
   - B) Manitoba
   - C) Nova Scotia
   - D) New Brunswick

3. The provincial governments are responsible for _____.
   - A) the post office
   - B) garbage collection
   - C) unemployment insurance
   - D) education

4. The municipal governments are responsible for _____.
   - A) RCMP
   - B) immigration
   - C) fire department
   - D) post office

5. Which Prime Minister was responsible for bringing the Constitution back to Canada?
   - A) Brian Mulroney
   - B) Pierre Trudeau
   - C) John A. Macdonald
   - D) Mackenzie King

6. Which province did not sign the Constitution Act, 1982?
   - A) Quebec
   - B) Newfoundland
   - C) Manitoba
   - D) British Columbia

7. Who was the first Prime Minister of Canada?
   - A) Sir John A. Macdonald
   - B) Wilfrid Laurier
   - C) Pierre Elliott Trudeau
   - D) Mackenzie King

8. Canada became an independent country in _____.
   - A) 1776
   - B) 1867
   - C) 1982
   - D) 1947

TRUE / FALSE

Circle T if the statement is true. Circle F if it is false.

1. The last province to join Confederation was Newfoundland. T / F

2. The federal government is responsible for education. T / F

3. The provincial government is responsible for recycling. T / F

4. The federal government is responsible for post offices. T / F

5. The municipal government is responsible for parking tickets. T / F

6. John A. Macdonald was responsible for bringing
   the Constitution back to Canada. T / F

7. Canada became an independent country in 1867. T / F

8. Saskatchewan joined Confederation in 1905. T / F

9. Nova Scotia joined Confederation in 1867. T / F

10. Manitoba joined Confederation in 1870. T / F

11. Sir Wilfrid Laurier was the first Prime Minister of Canada. T / F

FILL IN THE BLANKS

In the blank, write the word(s) needed to make the sentence complete.

1. Canada became an official country in _____.

2. _____ is the joining of provinces to make a new country.

3. _____ was the first Prime Minister of Canada.

4. Canadians celebrate Confederation on _____.

5. Remembrance Day is celebrated on _____.

6. Christmas is celebrated on _____.

7. New Year's Day is celebrated on _____.

8. Louis Riel was born in _____ (location).

9. Prime Minister _____ brought the Constitution back to Canada.

MATCHING

Match each province/territory with the year it joined Confederation. The blanks indicate how many provinces joined in each year.

A. British Columbia

B. Alberta

C. Saskatchewan

D. Manitoba

E. Ontario

F. Quebec

G. New Brunswick

H. Nova Scotia

I. Prince Edward Island

J. Newfoundland

K. Northwest Territories

L. Yukon

1870 ____ ____

1867 ____ ____ ____ ____

1905 ____ ____

1873 ____

1898 ____

1871 ____

1949 ____

Match each day with the correct date.

A. Canada Day

B. Christmas

C. Halloween

D. Valentine's Day

E. Remembrance Day

F. New Year's Day

G. St. Patrick's Day

I. Boxing Day

____ November 11

____ December 26

____ July 1

____ January 1

____ December 25

____ February 14

____ October 31

____ March 17

Which level of government is responsible for the following? Fill in the blank with the appropriate letter (F for federal, P for provincial or M for municipal). The first one has been done for you.

_F_ citizenship

____ utilities

____ education

____ recycling

____ currency

____ post office

    ___ highways   ___ immigration

    ___ garbage collection   ___ defence

    ___ unemployment insurance   ___ health care

SHORT ANSWER

Answer the following questions.

1. Which four provinces joined together to become Canada in 1867?

_____

2. What is the name of the national holiday of Canada?

_____

3. What is the *British North America Act*?

_____

4. Briefly describe who Louis Riel was and why he is important in Canada's history.

_____

5. Which two provinces entered into Confederation in 1905?

_____

6. What are the three levels of government in Canada?

_____

7. List three responsibilities of the federal government.

_____

8. List three responsibilities of the provincial government.

_____

9. List three responsibilities of the municipal government.

_____

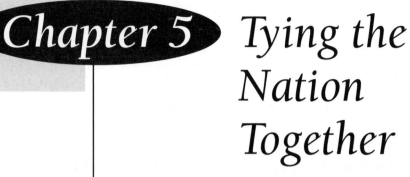

Chapter 5 Tying the Nation Together

SKILLS EMPHASIZED Reading comprehension, discussion, problem solving, expressing an opinion, explaining, reading a schedule, comparing and contrasting, making choices, sequencing, predicting.

PRE-READING I

- What is the most important form of transportation in the country you are from?

- Have you ever been on a train in Canada? If yes, where did you go?

- How far is it from Vancouver, British Columbia to St. John's, Newfoundland?

- How many people do you think it would take to build a railroad across Canada?

- What areas of Canada would be most difficult for building a railroad?

- How long do you think it took to build the railroad in Canada?

READING I: BUILDING THE RAILWAY, BUILDING THE COUNTRY

After Confederation in 1867, the government of Canada bought land owned by   *1*
the Hudson's Bay Company (parts of what are now Ontario, Quebec, Manitoba,
Saskatchewan, Alberta and the Northwest Territories). Prime Minister John A.
Macdonald wanted British Columbia to join Confederation. He also wanted settlers to move to the west. He and his government promised to build a railway that

CP Rail System

A ballast crew (hired by Onderdonk) at work beside Kamloops Lake, east of Savonas, 1883

Donald Smith (Lord Strathcona) driving the last spike in the CPR at Craigalachie

Provincial Archives of Alberta

History -- Geography   VISUAL TEACHING

"BIRTH OF THE WEST" History Teaching Pictures

The Art League

BUILDING of C.P.R. SERIES IX.

CRAIGALACHIE 1884
DONALD SMITH (LORD STRATHCONA) DRIVING THE LAST SPIKE IN C.P.R.

would go all the way to the Pacific ocean. It was extremely difficult to build the Canadian Pacific Railway. The rocky Canadian Shield in western Ontario and the mountains in Alberta and British Columbia made the job difficult and dangerous. To build the railway, the Canadian government hired a huge labour force, including 15 000 workers from China. They started working on the railroad in 1881. When it was finished in 1885, many Europeans began to move to the West.

2   The railway made long-distance travel possible. Wheat and other products could be easily transported. Although today most Canadians travel by car or plane, the railroads are still an important method of transporting goods.

COMPREHENSION AND DISCUSSION QUESTIONS

1. Why did Sir John A. Macdonald want to build the railroad?

2. How long did it take to build it?

3. Which parts of the railroad were the most difficult to build?

4. What were the advantages of having a railroad?

5. Some countries, for example, Japan, have trains which travel up to 200 kilometres an hour. Do you think Canada needs this type of train? If yes, where should these trains be located? Why?

LANGUAGE AND CONTACT ACTIVITIES

1. Transportation Quiz

Answer the following questions:

QUESTION	YES	NO
Have you ever been on a train in Canada?		
Do you drive a car?		
Have you ever been in an accident?		
Have you ever been on a boat on the ocean?		
Have you ever been on a plane? How many flights have you taken?		
Do you get nervous on planes?		
Do you ever get motion sickness?		
Do you know anyone who works in the transportation industry?		
Have you ever been on a subway?		
How do you get to class each day?		
What is your favourite way to travel?		

Compare your answers with those of a classmate. What do you and your partner have in common? How are you different?

2. Contributions of Immigrants

Immigrants built the railroad and in doing so, helped to ensure that British Columbia would join Confederation. What major contributions do immigrants make to Canada today? Work in pairs and share your list with others.

3. Win a Trip

You have decided to enter a contest to win a two-day vacation. You have to write a paragraph of 100 words explaining why you would like to take one of the following train trips: Toronto to Montreal, Ottawa to Kingston, or Edmonton to Jasper. The contest rules state that you must say why you want to go to the place you have chosen and why you want to take the train. Read your entry to the class. The class can decide who should win the trip.

PRE-READING II

- Before you came to Canada did you think it would be the same as or different from the USA?

- What do Canada and the USA have in common?

- What are the differences between Canada and the USA?

- Do you know if Canada and the USA have ever been at war against each other?

- Where would you rather live, Canada or the USA? Explain your answer.

READING II: CANADIAN AND AMERICAN RELATIONS

1 Sir John A. Macdonald wanted to build the railway to bring people to the west. He was afraid that the west would become part of the United States and it was his dream that Canada would stretch from sea to sea.

2 Canada and the United States have a great deal in common, but Canadians have always seen themselves as somewhat different from their American neighbours. When the USA became independent in 1776, many people who were loyal to the English King moved north to the Canadian colonies. About 40 000 loyalists came to Canada at this time.

3 In 1812 the USA went to war with England. The USA invaded the Canadian colonies because they belonged to England. The USA lost the

war. This was the only time that Canada and the USA were at war with each other. At the end of the war, the border between Canada and the USA was set at the 49th parallel. The large number of settlers who went west on the railroad in the late 1800s helped to make sure that the border never changed. Since that time, the United States and Canada have become close friends, although they occasionally have political disagreements. Today, Canada, the USA, and Mexico have signed an agreement that allows free trade across North America.

COMPREHENSION AND DISCUSSION QUESTIONS

1. What was Sir John A. Macdonald's dream?
2. What was he afraid of?
3. Who were the Loyalists? When did they come to Canada and why?
4. Have Canada and the USA ever been at war with each other? When? Who won?
5. Where is the border between Canada and the USA?
6. Do you think free trade with the United States will be good for Canada?
7. Do you think that Canada would ever go to war with the USA again?

LANGUAGE AND CONTACT ACTIVITIES

1. Newcomers' Difficulties

Imagine what it must have been like to have been one of the first pioneer families to come on the train to settle western Canada. As a class, discuss what problems would have faced a pioneer family. How are these difficulties different from or the same as the problems faced by newcomers today?

Order the difficulties of the pioneers, starting from the most difficult and going to least difficult.

2. Canada/USA Conflicts

Canada and the United States are good friends but sometimes they disagree. For example, Canadians get upset when Americans fish in their waters. As a class, list other problems between the two countries.

3. Canada in Conflict

Read the following chart:

CONFLICT	CONSEQUENCE FOR CANADA
Seven Year's War (1756–1763) between England and France	The French were defeated and England gained control of Canada
War of 1812, between Canada and the USA	The USA was defeated; the border between Canada & the USA was set.
The Riel Rebellion (1869–1870)	Louis Riel and his followers lost; Manitoba joined Confederation.
World War One (1914–1918)	Many Canadian soldiers died, protecting their allies in Europe.
World War Two (1939–1945)	Many Canadian soldiers died, protecting Europe's freedom. When the soldiers came home, so many of them married that they started a "baby boom."
The Korean Conflict (1950–1953)	Canadian soldiers died in this war.
Persian Gulf War (1991)	No Canadians died, but many others did.

In a group, discuss the following questions:

- Do you think Canada will ever be involved in another war?
- Do you think there will be a war within Canada?
- Have you been in a war?
- Do you think war is necessary?

CHINESE CANADIANS

Many Chinese men came to Canada in the nineteenth century to help build the railway. When it was completed a lot of them stayed, mostly in British Columbia. The federal government at the time would not allow the men to bring their families to Canada unless they paid a head tax. That is, they had to pay a lot of money for each family member. Most men could not afford the tax. Other laws prevented the Chinese from voting and taking certain jobs. It was not until 1947 that Chinese Canadians were given most of the rights enjoyed by other Canadians, but there were still restrictions on Chinese immigration that did not change until 1967. Canada has come a long way in the last few decades. There is now less discrimination. In 1988, David See-Chi Lam, a Vancouver businessman born in Hong Kong, was appointed to the position of lieutenant-governor (the Queen's representative) in the province of British Columbia.

JAPANESE CANADIANS

By the 1940s there were over 20 000 Japanese Canadians living in Canada. Most of these people lived in British Columbia. When Pearl Harbor was attacked by Japan in World War Two, the Canadian government sent Japanese Canadians to work camps in the interior of British Columbia and in Alberta. The government also sold all their property and possessions. After the war, many Japanese Canadians were deported to Japan. Others were relocated east of the Rockies. Some people spoke out against the government's policies and by 1949 Japanese Canadians' rights were restored. For several years the Japanese Canadian community tried to get the federal government to apologize for the discrimination during the war. In 1988, the federal government apologized and gave some money to those people who were discriminated against.

FOLLOW-UP

In one school, fourteen students in an ESL class were asked whether there is discrimination now in Canada. Nine people said that there is some discrimination on the basis of sex, skin colour, nationality, and language skills. How many people in your class have been discriminated against?

Here is a case of discrimination: Some religions require that people dress in a certain way; for example, Sikh men wear turbans. In 1994, some branches of the Royal Canadian Legion, which does not allow its members to wear headgear, decided not to let anyone inside wearing a turban. The Legion is a social club for war veterans and their families and friends. The Legion members argued that it is a sign of respect to remove headgear when entering the Legion. They say that allowing people to wear a turban would break an important tradition. What they were asking, however, was for turban wearers to break an important requirement of their religion in order to follow this tradition. Many Sikhs fought in World War Two and feel that they should have equal access to the Legion halls. Think of some other examples of discrimination in Canada. What do you think can be done about this problem?

Women in Canada have been fighting for equal rights for a long time. Do you think that women in Canada have the same job opportunities as men?

When ESL students were asked whether women should have equal rights, 12 out of 14 said yes; the two who said no were both men.

- Do you think that women *should* have equal rights?
- Do you think that women *do* have equal rights?
- In your class, is there a difference between the percentage of men and the percentage of women who think women should have equal rights?

Several years ago Svend Robinson, a Canadian MP (Member of Parliament) from British Columbia, announced openly that he is gay. Since then he has been re-elected several times. He is a very popular MP. Robinson has argued strongly for equal rights for gays and lesbians. In the last ten years there has been more acceptance of gays and lesbians, but they are still discriminated against by some people. Scientists estimate that approximately ten percent of all people are homosexual.

- Are people often openly gay or lesbian in your country?
- In your province are there laws to protect gay and lesbian people from discrimination?
- Why do you think people sometimes try to hide their sexual orientation?

GLOSSARY OF TERMS

NOUNS

agreement: in politics, a document in which countries share the same understanding about an issue

branch: a part of a large organization

contest: competition

contribution: donation

decade: 10 years

gay: homosexual

lesbian: a homosexual woman

labour force: workers

restriction: limit

Sikh: a person who belongs to a religion called Sikhism

subway: an underground train within a city

tradition: beliefs; customs from the past

turban: headgear; Sikh men must wear one

veteran: someone who has fought in a war

VERBS

to ensure: to make sure

to invade: to enter and attack

TEST YOURSELF

Tying the Nation Together

MULTIPLE CHOICE
Circle the best answer.

1. After Confederation, The Canadian government bought land from:
    A) the Americans   B) the Hudson's Bay Company
    C) Manitoba   D) the French

2. John A. Macdonald wanted to build the railway because _____.
    A) he needed to provide jobs   B) he wanted to unite Canada
    C) he liked trains   D) he wanted to travel

3. In 1812, Canada went to war with _____.
    A) Australia   B) France
    C) the United States   D) Bolivia

4. British Columbia joined Confederation because _____.
    A) people there preferred Canada over the United States
    B) It wasn't rich enough to become its own country
    C) people there wanted a train between the east and west
    D) none of the above

5. The work force used to build the Canadian Pacific Railway was largely made
    up of _____ workers.
    A) immigrant   B) women
    C) children   D) none of the above

TRUE/FALSE
Circle T if the statement is true. Circle F if it is false.

1. The Canadian Pacific Railway was started in 1885.   T / F

2. The Canadian Pacific Railway was finished in 1885.   T / F

3. The border between Canada and the USA is along the 60th parallel.   T / F

4. Many Loyalists moved to Canada after the American revolution.   T / F

5. Canada has had two conflicts with the United States.   T / F

6. Canada participated in both World War I and World War II   T / F

MATCHING

Canada has been involved in various conflicts throughout history. Match the following conflicts with the dates they began.

A. Korean Conflict   _____ 1991

B. World War I   _____ 1939

C. The Riel Rebellion   _____ 1756

D. War of 1812   _____ 1869

E. World War II   _____ 1914

F. Seven Year's War   _____ 1812

G. Persian Gulf War   _____ 1950

SHORT ANSWER

Answer the following questions.

1. Why did the government buy land owned by the Hudson's Bay Company?

_____

2. Why did John A. Macdonald want British Columbia to join Confederation?

_____

3. Why did John A. Macdonald want to build the Canadian Pacific Railway?

_____

4. Why was it difficult to build the Canadian Pacific Railway?

_____

5. List two things that the Canadian Pacific Railway was used for.

_____

6. Why did many people move to Canada from the United States after the American revolution of 1776?

_____

7. When was the border between Canada and the United States established?

_____

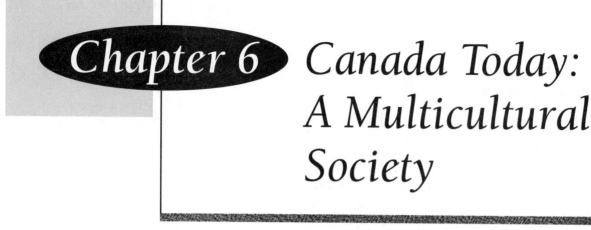

Chapter 6 — Canada Today: A Multicultural Society

SKILLS EMPHASIZED Reading comprehension, discussion, reading and constructing graphs, designing and conducting a survey, analyzing a survey, letter writing, listing, comparing and contrasting, explaining, reporting information, evaluating, expressing an opinion.

PRE-READING I: IMMIGRATION LEVELS TO CANADA

Look at the graph on page 69 and answer the following questions:

- 🙦 When was the period of greatest immigration to Canada?
- 🙦 When was the period of least immigration to Canada? Can you guess why?
- 🙦 Why do you think people came to Canada in the late 1800s?
- 🙦 Why do they come now?

READING I: IMMIGRATION TRENDS

1   There have been several times in Canadian history when large numbers of people came to this country to start a new life. In the late 1800s, following the completion

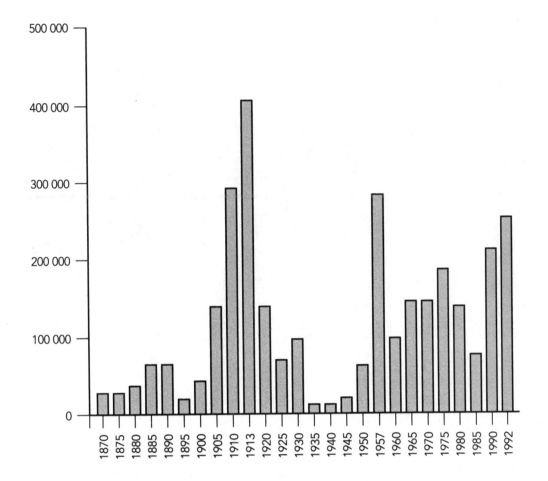

of the railway, the federal government encouraged Europeans to come to Western Canada to homestead (farm). Farmland was offered to settlers for free or for a very low price. Many Europeans came to the prairies to look for a better life. Other immigrants came to search for gold in British Columbia and Yukon. This period is considered the first big wave of immigration to Canada.

Just before the First World War (1914–1918), very large numbers of new- 2 comers arrived in Canada. In 1913 alone, more than 400 000 people came to this country. This was the second wave of immigration. After the Second World War (1939–1945), Canada's economy grew and people were needed to work in all the new jobs. This was the third period of high immigration to Canada.

Today there are still many people coming to Canada from other countries. 3 The graph on page 70 shows where immigrants came from in 1992.

This family came to western
Canada to homestead

Provincial Archives of Alberta

Immigration by source continent, 1992

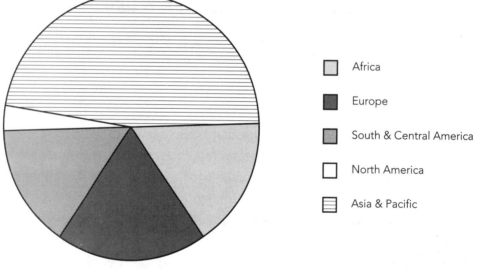

- Africa
- Europe
- South & Central America
- North America
- Asia & Pacific

COMPREHENSION AND DISCUSSION QUESTIONS

1. Why did many Europeans come to the west in the late 1800s?
2. When was the second period of high immigration to Canada?
3. Why do people immigrate to Canada today?
4. Why did you immigrate to Canada?
5. Where did the most immigrants come from in 1992?

Mining on Bonanza Creek, Yukon, during the Klondike gold rush

National Archives of Canada

LANGUAGE AND CONTACT ACTIVITIES

1. Categories of Immigrants

Immigration to Canada by class; 1994 plan

- Family Class
- Independent Immigrants
- Refugees

People immigrate to Canada in one of three categories: *family class* (newcomers who are joining family members already in Canada); *independent class* (immigrants who are chosen according to a point system, where points are given for occupation, language ability, education, work experience, financial status — this class includes business investors); and *refugee class* (these are people who might be in danger if they stayed in their own countries).

In pairs or groups, discuss the following questions:

- When you immigrated to Canada, did you come in the family class, independent or refugee category?
- Where were you when you applied to immigrate?
- How long did you have to wait?
- Could you choose where you wanted to go within Canada?
- Do you have any family here?
- Would you like to sponsor someone to come to Canada?

2. Changes to the Immigration Policy

In 1994, the federal government made some changes to the immigration policy. A greater percentage of newcomers will be in the independent class and fewer family class immigrants will be admitted to Canada. What do you think of this change?

3. Invite a Guest Speaker to Class

Working together, plan a letter. Invite an immigration official or settlement worker to come to your class to explain the immigration policy and to discuss how to sponsor an immigrant to Canada. Be sure to include your class time, dates, location, and the name and telephone number of a contact person from your class.

Make a list of questions that you would want to ask. For example,

- Who is eligible to sponsor an immigrant?
- How much does it cost?
- What are the sponsor's responsibilities?

4. Where Are the Students in Your Class from?

As a class, find out which countries all the students are from.

Write the names of the countries and the number of people from each one on the board.

Add up the total number of students in your class. Calculate the percentage of students from each country.

Example: The following percentages were taken from an ESL class in Vancouver:

There was a total of 20 students in the class.

Eight were from Hong Kong, $(8/20 = X/100, X = 40\%)$.

Thus 40% of the people in the class came from Hong Kong.

2 students came from Viet Nam = 10%

2 students came from Poland = 10%

3 students came from Korea = 15%

1 student came from Bosnia = 5%

1 student came from Sudan = 5%

2 students came from Romania = 10%

1 student came from India = 5%.

This pie graph shows the percentage of people from each country in the ESL class in Vancouver:

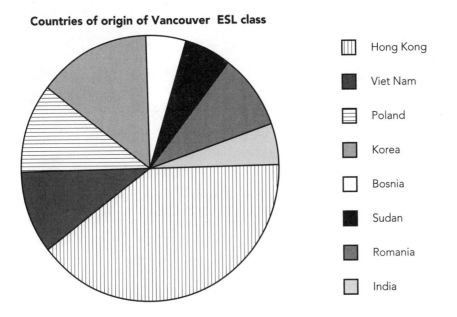

Countries of origin of Vancouver ESL class

Hong Kong

Viet Nam

Poland

Korea

Bosnia

Sudan

Romania

India

Now draw a pie graph of your class: Once you have found the percentage of students from every country in your class, draw a large circle on the board. Fill in the pie graph.

How is your class different from the sample ESL class in Vancouver?

PRE-READING II

🍃 Were you surprised at the number of people from different countries in Canada?

🍃 Are there many people from your country here?

🍃 Are there many people from different cultures in your former country?

Canada's people come from diverse backgrounds

Government of Canada

READING II: MULTICULTURALISM

1   In 1988 the Canadian Multiculturalism Act was passed. The Act states that the government of Canada respects and supports cultural and racial diversity. People are encouraged to keep and share their cultural and linguistic heritage. This means that all Canadians should have equal opportunities, no matter where they come from. They should also be able to celebrate their ethnic traditions and speak in their own language as well as English or French.

2   Canada is often called a cultural mosaic; a place where people from many countries can adapt to Canadian life and yet keep the traditions from their first culture. In the summer of 1991, the federal government surveyed Canadians. People were asked about their views on multiculturalism and about their attitudes toward different cultures in Canada. Here are some of the results from the survey:

- 🍃 61% of Canadians support the multiculturalism policy in Canada
- 🍃 73% believe that multiculturalism will provide greater equality for all Canadians
- 🍃 37% think that multiculturalism creates conflicts between groups
- 🍃 66% think that discrimination against non-whites is a problem
- 🍃 77% are against polygamy (marriage to more than one person at a time)
- 🍃 64% are against arranged marriages

- 51% believe that recent immigrants should have as much say about the future of Canada as people who were born and raised here.

- 95% believe that you can be proud to be a Canadian and be proud of your ancestry at the same time.

COMPREHENSION AND DISCUSSION QUESTIONS

1. What is the Multiculturalism Act?
2. What does it mean to say that Canada is a mosaic?
3. Do you agree with the Multiculturalism Act?
4. Do you think that the multiculturalism policy is good for Canada? Why or why not?
5. Do people from your first country maintain their heritage in Canada?
6. What do you think of arranged marriages?
7. If you have children, do you want them to carry on the traditions from their first country? If yes, do you think it will be difficult? Explain.

LANGUAGE AND CONTACT ACTIVITIES

1. Survey of Attitudes Toward Multiculturalism

Conduct a survey to find out what people think about multiculturalism. Each class member should ask five people (outside of class) to answer the following questions. Record their answers.

	YES	NO
1. Do you support the multiculturalism policy in Canada?		
2. Do you think that multiculturalism creates conflicts between groups?		
3. Do you think that discrimination against non-whites is a problem?		
4. Do you think that newcomers should have as much to say about the future of Canada as people who are born and raised here?		
5. Do you think that Canada should increase the level of immigration?		

As a class put your results from the survey together. How many people in total answered the survey? Calculate the percentage of people who answered yes or no to each of the questions and fill out the following chart:

QUESTION	%YES	%NO
Question 1		
Question 2		
Question 3		
Question 4		
Question 5		

Write a report of the results.

CONFLICT AND MULTICULTURALISM

Many people come to Canada because of conflict in their countries. They may have been at war with another country or with a particular group of people within their own country. Sometimes newcomers have trouble forgetting the hostility they feel towards the other group and continue to have conflict with members of that group here in Canada. In a survey conducted in Edmonton, ESL students were asked "What do you think about people bringing their conflicts to Canada?" Here are some examples of their comments:

"We live in Canada now. People who were our enemies are not our enemies here."
— woman from Iraq

"People come here to get away from war, not to make war."
— man from El Salvador

"We should find a middle way; there should be general rules for everyone, we must respect Canadian law."
— man from Romania

"It is bad to bring conflicts from your home country, people should get along even with their enemies here."
— woman from Bosnia

"Canada is a peaceful country, immigrants should respect that."
— woman from Korea

FOLLOW-UP

- ☙ Do you spend time outside of class with people from outside your own ethnic group?
- ☙ What do you think about bringing conflicts to Canada? Are there circumstances when it is okay?
- ☙ Do you think it is possible for enemies to become friends in a new country?
- ☙ Do you think that Canadian-born people understand the problems of newcomers?
- ☙ Do you think the government should provide money for ethnic celebrations?

GLOSSARY OF TERMS

NOUNS

ancestry: the cultural group from which you are descended

arranged marriage: a marriage where parents choose a husband or wife for their child

attitude: a way of feeling or thinking about someone or something

category: class or group

diversity: differences; variety

economy: the system by which a country's wealth is produced and used

heritage: cultural background

hostility: anger; animosity

mosaic: a collection of separate pieces that form a whole

policy: a course of action

trend: pattern

VERBS

to encourage: to support

to search: to look for

to sponsor: to pay for

to survey: to ask several questions of a number of people

ADJECTIVES

proud: feeling satisfaction and pleasure about something connected to oneself

TEST YOURSELF

Canada Today — A Multicultural Society

MULTIPLE CHOICE

Circle the best answer.

1. There were _____ waves of immigration to Canada.
   A) two   B) three
   C) four   D) five

2. The Canadian Multiculturalism Act was passed in _____.
   A) 1982   B) 1988
   C) 1867   D) 1905

3. Many of the immigrants who arrived in Canada during the first wave were

   _____.

   A) Chinese   B) African
   C) Australian   D) European

4. Immigrants can enter Canada under which of the following categories?
   A) family class   B) independent
   C) refugee   D) all of the above

5. The Canadian mosaic is a _____.
   A) traditional food dish
   B) traditional dance
   C) collection of distinct cultures
   D) political party

TRUE/FALSE

Circle T if the statement is true. Circle F if it is false.

1. Canada is often called a mosaic.   T / F

2. People came to Canada in the late 1800s to homestead.   T / F

3. Farmland was very expensive one hundred years ago.   T / F

4. An immigrant can enter Canada as an independent.   T / F

5. The highest number of immigrants entered Canada in 1945.   T / F

6. The majority of Canadians support immigration to Canada.   T / F

FILL IN THE BLANKS

In the blank, write the word(s) needed to complete the sentence.

1. The Canadian Multiculturalism Act was passed in _____.

2. Because of its multicultural nature, Canada is often called a

   _____.

3. The _____ wave of immigration occurred during the

   19th century.

4. _____ made up the majority of immigrants during the third

   wave of immigration.

SHORT ANSWER

1. Why did the federal government encourage large numbers of people to
   move to Western Canada in the 1800s?

   _____

2. Independent immigrants are chosen by a point system. List three things for
   which they are given points.

   _____

3. When was the greatest immigration to Canada?

   _____

4. Why did so many people come to Canada in the late 1800s?

   _____

5. List two reasons why the first immigrants came to Canada.

   _____

Chapter 7 What Do Canadians Do?

MATERIALS REQUIRED Classified section of the newspaper, sample résumés and cover letters, sample application forms, a few decks of cards.

SKILLS EMPHASIZED Reading comprehension, discussion, reading classified ads, letter writing, writing a résumé, sequencing, listing, giving instructions, making choices, explaining.

PRE-READING I

INDUSTRIAL DISTRIBUTION OF EMPLOYMENT (1987)	
Agriculture	4.0%
Other Primary Industries	3.4%
Manufacturing	17.0%
Construction	5.2%
Transportation, Communications & Other Utilities	7.6%
Trade with Other Countries	17.6%
Finance, Insurance, Real Estate	5.8%
Community Business & Personal Services	32.7%
Public Administration	6.7%

Adapted from Canada: A Portrait. Supply & Services Canada 1989

An aerial view of logs in the Queen Charlotte Islands

Government of Canada

- What kinds of jobs do the majority of working Canadians have?
- What is your job?
- Which category in the chart on page 80 fits your job?
- What is the main type of employment in your city or town? In your province?
- What kind of work did you do before you came to Canada?
- What is the main source of employment in the country you came from?
- Do you know people who make their living by farming? fishing? mining? trapping? logging? If so, where do they live?

READING I: WORKING LIFE IN CANADA

For hundreds of years, most people in Canada made their living from working with natural resources. Because much of the country is covered with trees, forestry is one of Canada's most important industries. Agriculture is important in all the provinces in Canada. Mining is done throughout the country, and large oil and gas deposits are found in Alberta, Saskatchewan and off the coast of Newfoundland. The Canadian fishing industry has always been important, but recently cod fishing off the Atlantic provinces has been stopped because there is a fear that all the fish will soon disappear.

Although much of Canada's economy still depends on agriculture, forestry, mining, oil refining, fishing, and manufacturing, most Canadians today live in

Telecommunications are becoming increasingly important

Government of Canada (Transmission line, Hearn Generating Station, Toronto)

cities and work in service occupations (office work, education, health, transportation, tourism, food services, etc.). In the future there will be more work in high technology industries. The fastest growing industries are in areas such as computers, communications, and medicine.

3   There have been several changes to the workplace in the last 25 years in Canada. One of the most important changes is the number of women who work outside the home.   A majority of adult women now have jobs. In more than half of all two-parent families, both parents work. Another change is that 25 years ago, a person could expect to stay in the same job for his or her whole career. Today, people often find that they have to change jobs several times before retirement. They may have to learn new skills as they change jobs. There are fewer jobs than in the past that require little education. Canada will need more workers who are well-educated. Also, now there are many more part-time jobs than ever before.

4   In the future, more and more people will work at home. The number of jobs which involve the use of computers is growing. Many people will not need to go to an office to do their work. Already some people do almost all of their work at home. They check with their office by telephone or by fax and they send their work to the office by computer.

5   Many immigrants to Canada don't know what kind of work they will find here. It is sometimes very difficult for them to get jobs in the same occupation they had in their own country. Immigrants who have been here for a long

A desktop publishing company in the owner Janet Schwegel's home

time have some advice for newcomers. They say that new immigrants need to be patient and persistent. It can be frustrating because most newcomers are underemployed in the beginning. They do not make as much money as they thought they would, and they are disappointed with the jobs they can find. However, many people eventually go back to school or find a job connected to their occupation.

COMPREHENSION AND DISCUSSION QUESTIONS

1. What are Canada's most important industries?
2. Why has cod fishing been stopped in the Atlantic provinces?
3. What kinds of jobs do most Canadians do today?
4. How has the role of women changed in the job market?
5. What kind of job would you like to have in Canada?
6. Do you need any extra education or training to get the job you want?

LANGUAGE AND CONTACT ACTIVITIES

1. Job Advertisements

Many people look for jobs in the classified ads in the newspaper. Some sample ads are shown on page 84.

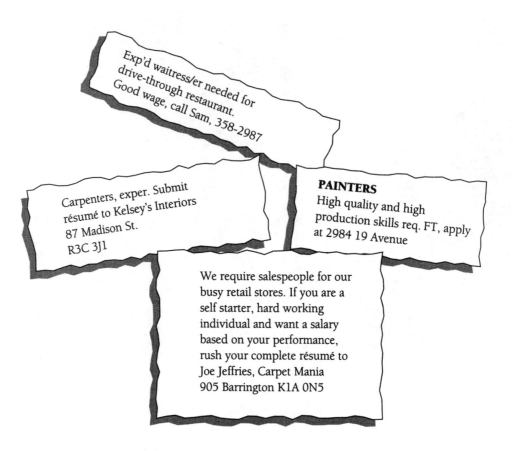

Exp'd waitress/er needed for drive-through restaurant. Good wage, call Sam, 358-2987

Carpenters, exper. Submit résumé to Kelsey's Interiors 87 Madison St. R3C 3J1

PAINTERS
High quality and high production skills req. FT, apply at 2984 19 Avenue

We require salespeople for our busy retail stores. If you are a self starter, hard working individual and want a salary based on your performance, rush your complete résumé to Joe Jeffries, Carpet Mania 905 Barrington K1A 0N5

- 🍂 What kinds of jobs are being advertised here?
- 🍂 How many of these jobs require experience?
- 🍂 How many jobs require a résumé?
- 🍂 Do you think these jobs pay well? Explain your answer.
- 🍂 Which job do you think pays the most? Why?
- 🍂 Do you qualify for any of these jobs?

2. Finding a Job

Find the classified ad section in your paper.

- 🍂 What kinds of jobs are available?
- 🍂 Some newspapers have a special section called a careers section. What is the difference between the jobs advertised in the careers section and the jobs in the classifieds?

3. Writing a Cover Letter and a Résumé

Look again at the job ads in your newspaper. Pick one that asks for a résumé. Write a cover letter and a résumé to apply for the job, following the examples given here:

SAMPLE COVER LETTER

Rodrigo Sanchez
6 — 83 Oak Drive
Ottawa ON
K1A 2Z3

September 22, 1995

Joe Jeffries
Carpet Mania
905 Barrington
Ottawa ON
K1A 0N5

Dear Mr. Jeffries:

I would like to apply for the job of salesperson for Carpet Mania. I have enclosed my résumé. I am a hard worker and I think I could make a good contribution to your store. I look forward to hearing from you.

Sincerely,

Rodrigo Sanchez

SAMPLE RÉSUMÉ

Rodrigo Sanchez
6 — 83 Oak Drive
Ottawa ON
K1A 2Z3

Education:

(list the years, the training and the schools that you attended)

Work Experience:
(list all relevant work experience, dates, name of company, location and job responsibilities)

Skills:
(list any skills you have that will help you on the advertised job)

References:
(list the names, addresses and phone numbers of two or three people who can say that you are a good worker. The best references are former employers, but if you do not have a former employer in Canada, ask your teacher)

---

4. Filling Out an Application Form

Many employers ask people to fill out application forms. These forms are different from one company to the next, but they all ask for your name and address, your social insurance number (SIN), your previous education and work experience. Fill out the sample form on page 87 with your personal information.

APPLICATION FORM

Personal Information

Name: _____   SIN: _____

Address: _____

      apt. #   street

_____

      city   province   postal code

Tel. # (h) _____ (b) _____

Previous Education

Schools Attended	Location (city, country)	Month/Year from to	Degree

Previous Employment

Name, Address, Tel. # of Employer   Job Dates Reason for Leaving

_____

_____

_____

_____ Signature _____ Date

5. Minimum Wage in Canada

Choose one person in the class to call Canada Employment. Find out what the minimum wage is in your province. Is there a minimum wage in your former country? Is it more or less than the minimum wage in your province?

PRE-READING II

- ❧ Do you play any sports?
- ❧ Do you have any hobbies?
- ❧ Have you ever been to a hockey game?
- ❧ Have you ever bought a lottery ticket? If yes, have you ever won anything?

A skier enjoying winter

Government of Canada

READING II: LEISURE LIFE IN CANADA

1   Canadians enjoy the outdoors. In the summertime, people like to swim, fish, garden, bicycle, and walk. Many people go camping and hiking for a few days in a provincial or national park. In the winter a lot of people skate, toboggan, or ski. But the most popular winter sport is hockey; some people play it but many more watch it on TV. Watching television is the most popular leisure activity of all. On average, Canadians watch more than three hours of TV a day.

2   Another very popular activity is gambling. Some people buy lottery tickets and dream of what they will do if they win the jackpot. Other people go to casinos or bingo halls and play to win. Most of the time they actually lose more money than they make, but they have a good time.

COMPREHENSION AND DISCUSSION QUESTIONS

1. What is the most popular leisure activity in Canada?

2. What are some sports that people play in the winter? In the summer?

3. What are three types of gambling that Canadians like?

4. Have you ever bought a lottery ticket?

5. What would you do if you won a million dollars?

6. Have you tried any winter sports here in Canada?

7. Do you watch hockey on TV?

8. Are there any TV programs in your first language in your city or town?

9. What is your favourite leisure activity?

LANGUAGE AND CONTACT ACTIVITIES

1. Card Game

Many Canadians like to play cards or board games such as *Scrabble*. They often start when they are very little. A popular card game that parents play with their children is called *Go Fish*. This game can be played by two or more people. Here are the instructions for playing *Go Fish*:

1. Shuffle the deck.

2. Deal seven cards to each player.

3. Look at your cards; then sort them by number, for example, put all the 6s together and all the Kings together.

4. If you have four of any number, put them face up on the table.

    Now you are ready to play. The goal of the game is to get complete sets of a number (all four), put the sets down, and run out of cards before anyone else.

5. Ask any other player for a card that you want, for example, "Do you have any 8s"? You can only ask for cards that you have at least one of.

6. If the other player has the cards you ask for, he or she has to give them to you and you can ask for something else. If the other player does not have the cards you asked for, he or she says "Go fish." You then draw a new card from the deck.

7. The next player takes his or her turn.

    The game ends when one person has put down all his or her cards and has no cards left.

    Write a set of instructions for a game or sport that you played in the country you came from. Show the students in the class how to play this game.

2. Camping

You are going to go camping for two days. It is the middle of the summer. In pairs, decide the following: Where will you go? What items will you bring with you? What kind of food will you bring?

Canadians camping in the great outdoors

Robert H. Short

THE CHANGING FACE OF CANADA

- Over the last few decades there has been a rise in the divorce rate. Single-parent and blended families are becoming very common. Some children may grow up with several step-relations in their lives while others live with only one parent.

- More women are working outside the home than ever before. As a result, there is a great need for daycare for children.

- Although the law says that people should not be discriminated against because of age, many workplaces now require that their employees retire at age 65. This is called mandatory retirement. Employers say that they need to make room for new, younger people in the workplace.

- Although there are many different religions represented in Canada (Judaism, Islam, Buddhism, etc.), Christianity has the most members. In the last few decades the traditional Christian churches (Catholic, Anglican, Presbyterian, United) have lost significant numbers of members. Many Canadians say that they have religious beliefs, but they are not interested in going to a place of worship (e.g., a church).

- Thirty years ago, Canadians thought the outlook for health was a very good one. With the development of antibiotics and vaccines many diseases were eliminated. Today the picture doesn't look so good. Many viruses and bacteria have become resistant to drugs. In addition, new diseases have emerged. The worst of these is AIDS, which at this time has no cure.

FOLLOW-UP

- Why do you think that more and more Canadians are getting divorced?

- Do you think married couples should stay together no matter what?

- Do you think the government should provide funds for daycare, or is it an individual responsibility?

- Do you think that requiring people to retire at age 65 is discrimination? Why or why not?

- Why do you think fewer people are going to church?

- Do you think we will see many new diseases in the future?

GLOSSARY OF TERMS

NOUNS

career: the general course of a person's working life

leisure time: time when a person is not working; free time

oil refining: processing oil to make it usable

reference: the name of a person who can speak on one's behalf

résumé: a statement of a person's work experience and educational qualifications

retirement: the end of one's career

technology: the application of scientific knowledge

underemployed: having a job which does not make use of one's skills and education

VERBS

to look forward to: to anticipate; to be excited about

ADJECTIVES

frustrating: maddening; disappointing

patient: willing to wait

persistent: continuing to try despite opposition

TEST YOURSELF

What Do Canadians Do?

TRUE/FALSE

Circle T if the statement is true. Circle F if it is false.

1. Agriculture is an important industry in Canada today.   T / F

2. In most Canadian families, only one of the two parents work.   T / F

3. Many Canadians today have more than one job before they retire.   T / F

4. More people will work at home in the future.   T / F

5. Jobs in Canada in the future will require more advanced education.   T / F

6. Single parent families are not very common in Canada.   T / F

7. Fewer women have jobs now than before.   T / F

8. Most Canadians like going to a place of worship.   T / F

SHORT ANSWER

Answer the following questions.

1. List two natural resources found in British Columbia.

_____

2. List two industries found in Prince Edward Island.

_____

3. List two industries found in Quebec.

_____

4. List two main industries in Alberta.

_____

5. List two main industries in Ontario.

_____

6. List two main industries in New Brunswick.

_____

7. What is one of the most important changes that has happened in the workplace in Canada?

_____

8. List four activities that Canadians enjoy doing in the summer.

_____

9. List four activities that Canadians enjoy doing in the winter.

_____

10. What religion has the most members in Canada?

_____

Chapter 8 — How is Canada Governed?

MATERIALS REQUIRED List of local MPs, MLAs, and council members; pictures of politicians.

SKILLS EMPHASIZED Reading comprehension; discussion; matching; expressing opinions; evaluating; organizing; letter writing.

PRE-READING I

- What do you know about the federal government?
- Who is the Prime Minister of Canada?
- What is the name of the party in power?
- Do you know who your own Member of Parliament (MP) is?
- How do people become Members of Parliament?
- Who is the Lieutenant Governor in your province?
- Who is the Premier of your province?
- Who is your Mayor?

READING I: THE STRUCTURE OF GOVERNMENT

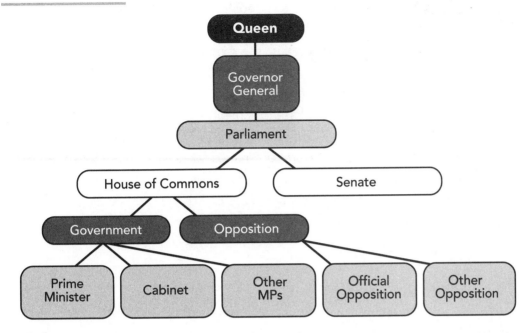

Doug Engel

Queen Elizabeth II is the head of Canada. She is represented by the Governor General of Canada and the Lieutenant Governors of each province.

The Federal Government

1 The federal government is called Parliament. Parliament consists of the Crown (Queen or King), the House of Commons and the Senate. Today Queen Elizabeth II is the head of Canada. Because she lives in England, she has a representative in Canada who performs her duties. Her representative is called the Governor General. The people in the House of Commons are elected by the people of Canada. They are called Members of Parliament (MPs). The people in the Senate are chosen (appointed) by the Prime Minister. They are called Senators.

Government of Canada

2   Members of Parliament in the House of Commons represent the people who elected them. Each MP usually belongs to a political party. After an election, the party that has the most MPs forms the government. The leader of that party is the Prime Minister. The party with the second most MPs elected forms the Official Opposition. Their leader is the Leader of the Opposition. MPs from other parties are also opposition members.

3   The Prime Minister chooses MPs (and sometimes Senators) to give advice and help. These people are called Cabinet Ministers. The Cabinet Ministers have special jobs. For example, the Minister of Finance takes care of the government's money. There are many people who work for the Cabinet Ministers. They are a part of the civil service. The people who work in the civil service are not elected. They apply for jobs with the government the same way that people apply for jobs with businesses.

Provincial Governments

4   Provincial governments are very similar to the federal government, except they have no Senate. The Crown is represented by a Lieutenant Governor. Each province has a legislative assembly which is similar to the federal House of Commons. The Members of the Legislative Assembly (MLAs) are elected by the people in the province. Usually members belong to a political party. After an election, the leader of the party with the most elected MLAs becomes the Premier of the province. The leader of the party with the second most votes becomes the Leader of the Opposition. The Premier of the province chooses Cabinet Ministers to look after provincial government departments (for example, Education).

Municipal Governments

5   People in cities and towns vote for a local or municipal government. Usually the head of the municipal government is called the Mayor and other members of this government are called Council Members or Aldermen. These people meet regularly to discuss local issues and make local laws (called bylaws).

COMPREHENSION AND DISCUSSION QUESTIONS

1. Who is the official head of Canada's government?
2. Who represents the Queen in the federal government?
3. Parliament is made up of two parts. What are they?

4. What is the difference between them?

5. How is the Prime Minister chosen?

6. What do Cabinet Ministers do?

7. What is the civil service? Do you know anyone who works in the civil service? If yes, what does he or she do?

LANGUAGE AND CONTACT

ACTIVITIES

POLITICAL PARTIES

A political party is a group of people who share the same ideas about what the government should do. There are several political parties in Canada (the Liberal party, the Reform party, the New Democratic party, the Bloc Quebecois, the Progressive Conservative party, the National party, the Communist party of Canada, the Green party, etc.). Each party has a leader. The leader of the party with the largest number of elected MPs is the Prime Minister. Some MPs do not belong to a party. They are called Independents.

1. Federal Government Matching Exercise

Match the words on the left with the definitions on the right. The first one has been done for you.

1.	Governor General	_10_	one of the parts of Parliament
2.	Prime Minister	____	an appointed government official
3.	Senator	____	a group of MPs with special responsibilities
4.	Federal government	____	Queen's representative
5.	MP	____	Leader of party with the most MPs
6.	Official Opposition	____	an elected government official
7.	Queen	____	Government of Canada
8.	Political party	____	Head of Canada
9.	Cabinet	____	Party with the second largest number of MPs
10.	House of Commons	____	Group of people who share ideas about how to run the country

2. Find Out Who Is in the Government

Find the answers to the following questions by calling the electoral officer in your city or town or invite a politician to your class:

- Who is the Governor General of Canada?
- Who is the Prime Minister?
- Which political party does the Prime Minister belong to?
- Who is the leader of the Official Opposition?
- Which political party does that person belong to?
- Who is your MP?
- What party does he or she belong to?
- Who is your MLA?
- What party does he or she belong to?
- Who is the Premier of your province?
- What political party does he or she lead?
- Who is the Mayor of your town?

3. Develop a Chart of the Provincial Government

Look at the chart of the federal government at the beginning of *Reading I*. Using the information in *Reading I*, draw a similar chart of the provincial government.

4. The Queen

Do you think that Canada needs a Queen? Do you think that Canada should appoint a Head of State from within the country? Explain your answers.

PRE-READING II

- How are laws made in your country of origin?
- Do you know how laws are made in Canada?
- Who makes the laws in Canada?
- How can laws be changed?

READING II: PASSING A LAW IN THE FEDERAL GOVERNMENT

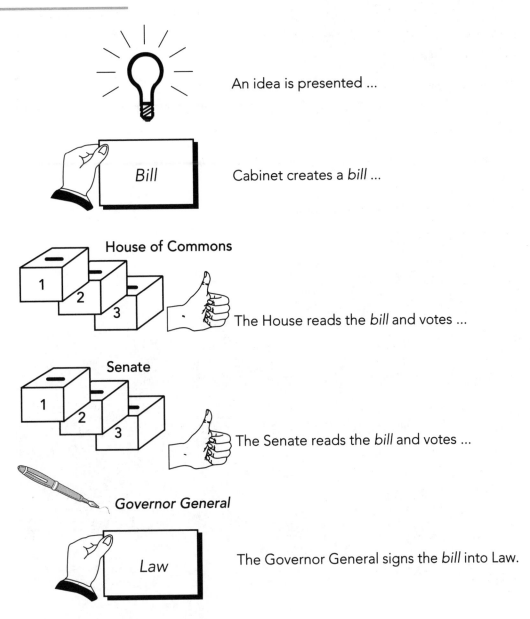

An idea is presented ...

Cabinet creates a *bill* ...

The House reads the *bill* and votes ...

The Senate reads the *bill* and votes ...

The Governor General signs the *bill* into Law.

Doug Engel

In Canada, all federal laws are made in Parliament. Any MP or Senator can suggest a new law. First they write an idea down on paper — this is called a *bill*. All the MPs read the bill three times and talk about it. After the third reading they vote *Yes* or *No*. The bill is also read three times in the Senate. If a majority of MPs and Senators vote *Yes* for the bill, the Governor General signs the bill. This is called royal assent. The bill is now a law or an Act of Parliament.

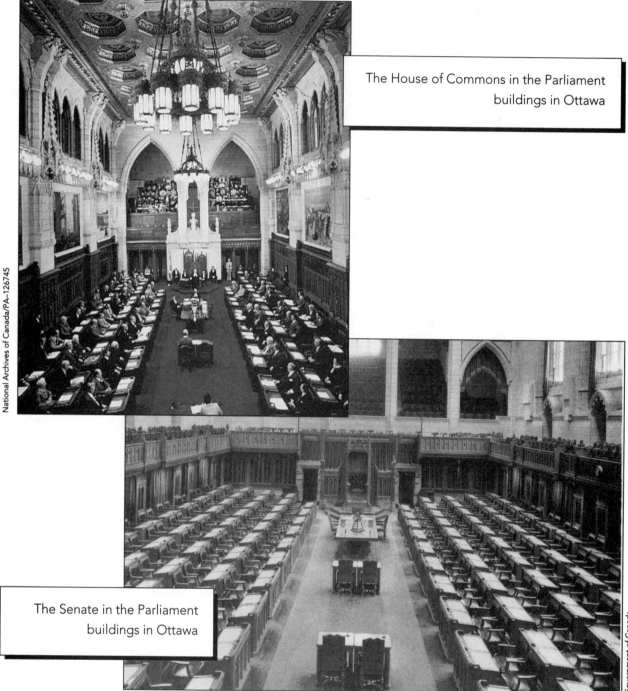

National Archives of Canada/PA–126745

The House of Commons in the Parliament
buildings in Ottawa

The Senate in the Parliament
buildings in Ottawa

Government of Canada

In provincial governments, the procedure is similar, except there is no senate. After a bill has gone through three readings in the Legislature, the politicians vote on the proposed change. If the vote passes, the Lieutenant Governor signs the bill and it becomes a law.

COMPREHENSION AND DISCUSSION QUESTIONS

1. Who can suggest a new law? What is it called before it becomes a law?
2. How many times does the House of Commons discuss a bill?
3. Who gives a federal law royal assent?
4. What new laws would you like to see in Canada?
5. Are there any laws that you would like to change (for example, immigration)?

LANGUAGE AND CONTACT ACTIVITIES

1. Choose a side on a Canadian issue

There are a number of controversial issues in Canada today. Some people would like to see changes in the laws that relate to capital punishment, abortion, and the right to die. Choose one of these issues. Find out what the law says about the issue you have chosen. Divide the class into two groups — one for the issue, the other against. For example, one group will take the view that capital punishment should be reinstated while the other group will argue that there is no need for capital punishment. Work together to plan your arguments. Try to use information from the newspaper to support your arguments. Then debate your points.

2. Field Trip

Plan a trip to see government at work. If you live in a capital city, phone your legislature to arrange for a tour. If you don't live in a capital city, phone your municipal government and arrange for a tour of city hall.

3. Group Discussion

In groups, discuss the following questions:

- Do you think the federal government is doing a good job? Why or why not?
- What do you think Canada's biggest problem is?
- What would you do if you were the Prime Minister?
- What do you think the biggest problem is in your province or territory?
- What would you do if you were the Premier?
- What do you think the biggest problem in your city or town is?
- What would you do if you were Mayor?

4. Write to a politician

As a class choose an issue about which you would like to see a change in the law. It may be taxes, immigration, health care, abortion, or something else. Then, in pairs, discuss what you would like the government to do about this issue. Write a letter to a politician in the level of government (an MP, MLA or Councillor) responsible for that issue. Use these guidelines to write your letter:

🍂 Clearly say what the issue is.

🍂 Clearly say how and why you would like to see the law changed regarding this issue.

🍂 Ask for a reply.

🍂 Keep your letter short.

🍂 Be polite.

TAXES IN CANADA

Canadians sometimes feel that they are the most taxed nation in the world. Every year, people who have earned money pay income tax to both the federal and the provincial governments. People who own a house pay property taxes to the municipal government. Also, everyone pays an extra tax on their purchases (GST). When the GST (Goods and Services Tax) was first introduced, the Canadian public protested very strongly, but the government started charging the GST anyway. In addition to the GST, all provinces except Alberta have a provincial sales tax on most items. These are all taxes that people can see. There are also hidden taxes, such as the taxes on cigarettes, gas and alcohol. Traditionally, taxes were created to pay for services for Canadian people such as health care, unemployment insurance, Canada pension, education, welfare, the upkeep of roads, etc. Today, many governments are cutting back on the services, but taxes keep going up.

FOLLOW-UP

When an ESL class was asked what surprised them most about Canada, several people said that they were shocked at how high the taxes are here.

🍂 Do you think taxes are too high?

🍂 Do you think the government wastes money?

- Would you be willing to pay higher taxes for more services?

- Which are the areas where you think government should spend the most money: defence, scientific research, transportation, health care, education, other?

- If the governments were to cut taxes further, which services could you live without?

- Are there any government services in Canada that are important to you that you did not have in your country of origin?

- Do you think too many or too few services are provided by the governments? Explain your answer.

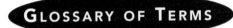

GLOSSARY OF TERMS

NOUNS

abortion: the termination or ending of a pregnancy

capital punishment: punishment by death for a crime

controversial issue: an issue on which people have conflicting opinions and views

procedure: a way of doing things

representative: a person who has been chosen to act in place of another

right to die: the right to choose to end one's own life

VERBS

to reinstate: to bring back a law

TEST YOURSELF

How is Canada Governed?

MULTIPLE CHOICE

Circle the best answer.

1. The federal government consists of the following:
   A) MPs, Senators, Aldermen
   B) Crown, Lieutenant Governor, House of Commons
   C) Governor General, MPs, Senators
   D) Prime Minister, Cabinet Ministers, MLAs

2. The Prime Minister appoints _____.
   A) MPs
   B) Cabinet Ministers
   C) the civil service
   D) Premiers

3. Royal assent occurs when _____.
   A) the Governor General signs a bill
   B) the Mayor signs a bill
   C) the bill is sent to the Senate
   D) the Prime Minister signs a bill

4. The Governor General is the Queen's representative for the _____ government.
   A) federal
   B) provincial
   C) municipal
   D) all of the above

5. The Lieutenant Governor is the Queen's representative for the _____ government.
   A) federal
   B) provincial
   C) municipal
   D) all of the above

6. The House of Commons reads a bill _____ time[s].
   A) zero
   B) one
   C) two
   D) three

7. The three levels of government in Canada are the _____.
   A) federal, provincial, national
   B) federal, Senate, civil service
   C) local, provincial, municipal
   D) federal, provincial, municipal

8. The official head of Canada's government is the _____.
   A) Prime Minister   B) Cabinet Minister
   C) Queen   D) Lieutenant Governor

9. The Prime Minister of Canada is _____.
   A) the person who gets the most votes
   B) the leader of the party that gets the most votes
   C) the leader of the party with the most elected MPs
   D) appointed by the House of Commons

10. The federal Parliament is made up of _____.
    A) House of Commons, Senate
    B) Governor General, Prime Minister
    C) Government, Official Opposition
    D) Prime Minister, Cabinet

11. The provincial government is made up of _____.
    A) the Prime Minister   B) MLAs
    C) Cabinet Ministers   D) Councillors

TRUE / FALSE

Circle T if the statement is true. Circle F if it is false.

1. The people in the House of Commons are not elected.   T / F

2. The people in the Senate are not elected by
   the people of Canada.   T / F

3. People who work in the civil service are elected.   T / F

4. Provincial governments have a Senate.   T / F

5. The Queen is represented in the municipal government.   T / F

6. Only a Member of Parliament can introduce a new law.   T / F

7. The Governor General must sign a bill
   before it becomes law.   T / F

FILL IN THE BLANKS

In the blank, write in the word(s) needed to complete the sentence.

1. The present Prime Minister of Canada is _____.

2. There are _____ levels of government in Canada.

3. The people in the _____ are appointed by the Prime Minister.

4. The party that has the most MPs elected is the _____.

5. The party that has the second most MPs elected is the _____.

6. The leader of the party with the most MPs elected is the

    _____.

7. The equivalent of the federal House of Commons in the provincial

    governments is the _____.

8. The leader of a provincial government is called the _____.

9. Municipal government is made up of the _____ and several

    _____.

10. When a new law is suggested and written down, it is called a

    _____.

11. _____ is when a bill is signed by the Governor General.

MATCHING

Match the following words with the appropriate definition.

A. Prime Minister	_____ The Queen's representative in the provincial government
B. Governor General	_____ Appointed by the Prime Minister
C. Lieutenant Governor	_____ The leader of the party with the most MLAs elected
D. MLA	_____ The leader of the party with the most MPs elected
E. Official Opposition	_____ A person who is elected to the provincial government

F. Senator   _____ The Queen's representative
in the federal government

G. Premier   _____ The party with the second
most MPs or MLAs elected

H. MP   _____ A person who is elected to
the federal government

SHORT ANSWER

Answer the following questions.

1. What is the role of the Governor General?

_____

2. Who are the Members of Parliament?

_____

3. How are Members of Parliament chosen?

_____

4. How are Senators chosen?

_____

5. How does Canada determine who will be Prime Minister?

_____

6. What is the role of a Cabinet Minister?

_____

7. What is the role of the Lieutenant Governor?

_____

8. How does a person become the Premier of a province?

_____

9. What is a "bill"?

_____

10. What does "royal assent" mean?

_____

11. Who is the MP in your area?

_____

12. Who is the MLA in your area?

_____

13. Who is the Mayor of your community?

_____

Chapter 9 Elections

MATERIALS REQUIRED Voter's kit, including sample ballots; pictures of campaigning, lawn signs.

SKILLS EMPHASIZED Reading comprehension, discussion, sequencing, identifying, making choices, expressing opinions.

PRE-READING

- Have you ever voted before?
- Who can vote in your country of origin?
- Do you think you will vote in the next election in Canada?
- How do you decide who to vote for?
- Would you like to be a politician?
- Do you know what a ballot is?

READING: ELECTIONS

Canada is a representative democracy. This means that we elect people to make the laws for us. At least every five years the Prime Minister calls an election for the federal government and the Premier of the province calls an election for the province. Municipal elections are usually held every three years. In a federal election, the country is divided into approximately 295 sections (called ridings or constituencies).

1

The people who live in a riding vote for one person to represent them in the government as an MP. In each riding voters can choose between several candidates who represent different political parties.

Before the Election

2 Once the Prime Minister has announced an election date, the people who can vote in each riding have to be counted and put on a voters' list. This is done to make sure that no one votes twice and to make sure that only people who are eligible actually vote.

Who is Eligible to Vote in Canada?

3 🐦 Canadian citizens who are over 18
🐦 Citizens who have lived outside Canada for less than five years
🐦 Citizens outside Canada who work for the government

4 To make up the voters' list, the government hires enumerators to count eligible voters. Enumerators are people who go from door to door asking questions to find out who can vote. They record the name, address, age, and citizenship status of all eligible voters living in each place they visit. Then they send a notice of enumeration card to eligible voters. This card tells the voters where and when to vote.

5 Before voting, the people in a riding decide which candidate's ideas they like best. They also decide which party they like best. Voters can find out what candidates think by watching TV, reading the newspaper, going to party meetings, and reading brochures.

Election Day

6 On the day of the election, people go to a place in their neighbourhood called a polling station where they vote. When they arrive at the polling station, they give their names to a poll clerk who checks to see that they are on the voters' list. The voters' names are crossed off the list and they are each given a ballot. A ballot is a list of the candidates and their parties running in the election. An example of a typical ballot is shown on the next page.

7 Voters go to polling booths — private places where they can vote without anyone seeing the ballot. The voters put an X beside the name of the person they want to be MP and then they fold the ballot. Each ballot is then put into a locked box. In Canada, voting is by secret ballot. In other words, voters don't have to tell anyone who they voted for if they don't want to. Also the poll clerks

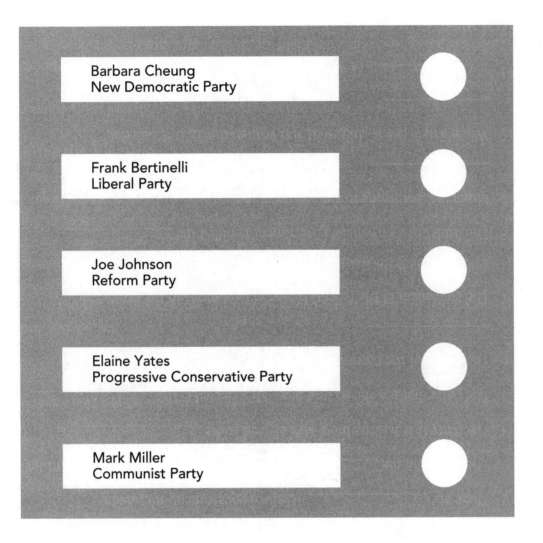

never look at the ballots when the voters put them in the box. There are people called scrutineers who make sure that voting is done properly.

At 8:00 p.m. in every province, the polls close. The votes are then counted *8* and the Chief Electoral Officer announces the winners in each riding.

After the Election

After the votes are counted across Canada, the new government is announced. *9* Each person who wins in a riding becomes a Member of Parliament (MP) and goes to the House of Commons in Ottawa. MPs usually fly or drive back and forth between their ridings and their offices in Ottawa. The party that has the largest number of elected MPs becomes the government. The leader of that party becomes the Prime Minister of Canada. The party with the second largest number of elected MPs become the Official Opposition. Other parties with elected MPs are also called opposition parties.

A candidate and his supporters in an election campaign

Margie McCaffery

COMPREHENSION AND DISCUSSION QUESTIONS

1. How often are federal, provincial, and municipal elections held?

2. What is a riding?

3. Who calls an election?

4. How do you get your name on a voters' list?

5. How can you decide who to vote for?

6. Why is voting done by secret ballot?

7. After an election, how is the Prime Minister chosen?

8. Can you suggest a better system for running an election?

WHO SHOULD YOU VOTE FOR?

Candidates who run in an election are usually nominated by the party they belong to. There are often several candidates from different parties running in the same riding. For example, in your riding there may be a Liberal, a Conservative, a Reform, an NDP, a Communist, and a Green party candidate. Each candidate tries to get your vote by campaigning. This means that the candidate may come to your house to talk to you, appear on television and radio, express his or her views at community centres and put signs up all over the riding. You may also get brochures about the candidate and the ideas of the party (party platform) in your mailbox. It is your responsibility to find out as much as you can about all of the candidates and the parties they represent in your riding. Then you can choose the candidate whose ideas you like the best.

In 1993, Jean Chrétien became the Prime Minister of Canada

Office of the Prime Minister

LANGUAGE AND CONTACT ACTIVITIES

1. The Voting Process

Read the following steps involved in the voting process. Put them in the right order and number them from 1–12.

- The voter goes to a polling booth and votes.
- Voters go to the polling station to vote.
- Political parties start to campaign.
- The voter's name is crossed off the list and the voter is given a ballot.
- The votes are counted.
- The government hires enumerators to count eligible voters
- The ballot is put into a locked box.
- Eligible voters receive a notice of enumeration card in the mail.
- The winners of the election are announced.
- Enumerators go from door to door.
- The voters' list is published.
- The Prime Minister calls an election.

2. Canadians' Concerns

Look in the Letters to the Editor section of your newspaper. What kinds of issues are people concerned about? Write some of these issues on the board. Pick one issue. What viewpoints do you and your classmates have on the issue?

3. Role Play an Election

As a class, choose two or more students to act as candidates who are running in an election. They have to take a side on one of the issues you have identified in the newspaper. They must try to convince the class to vote for them because of their views on the issue.

Make ballots using the names of the class candidates. Choose one person to be the poll clerk. The poll clerk can give the ballots to each person in the class. Now vote. Don't show your ballot to anyone else. Fold your ballot and give it back to the poll clerk. After everyone has voted, the poll clerk counts the votes. The candidate with the most votes wins.

MAJORITY AND MINORITY GOVERNMENTS

After the votes are counted, parties look to see who had the most elected MPs. If a party has the most MPs and also has more than half of all the MPs in the House of Commons, they form a *majority* government. This means that when there is a vote in the house, the government always has more people on their side than all the opposition members together. Sometimes, after an election, there are more MPs in opposition parties than in the government. In this case the government is called a *minority* government. They will have a hard time passing laws because all the opposition members may vote against them. Also, the opposition parties can call for a vote of non-confidence. This means that all the MPs vote on whether the minority government should stay in power or a new election should be called.

FOLLOW-UP

Find out how many seats each party in the House of Commons has today. Is there a minority or a majority government?

Some democracies have only two political parties; that way, there is never a minority government. Do you think it is better to have many parties or to have only two parties? Explain your answer.

GLOSSARY OF TERMS

NOUNS

brochure: a pamphlet which provides information

candidate: a person who runs in an election

eligible: fulfilling necessary conditions

enumerator: a person who counts voters

VERBS

to elect: to choose by voting

TEST YOURSELF

Elections

MULTIPLE CHOICE

Circle the best answer.

1. Federal elections are held about every _____ years.
   - A) 5
   - B) 3
   - C) 2
   - D) 6

2. Who calls an election in Canada?
   - A) the Prime Minister
   - B) the Governor General
   - C) the Queen
   - D) the MPs

3. What do enumerators do?
   - A) count numbers
   - B) count voters
   - C) count candidates
   - D) count MPs

4. Canadians must be _____ years old in order to vote.
   - A) 12
   - B) 16
   - C) 18
   - D) 21

5. A majority government has _____.
   - A) fewer seats than the official opposition
   - B) the same number of seats as the opposition
   - C) more seats than all the other opposition parties combined

6. Enumerators record the following except _____.
   - A) name
   - B) address
   - C) age
   - D) religion

7. All of the following are eligible to vote in Canada, except
   - A) Canadian citizens under 18
   - B) citizens outside Canada who work for the government
   - C) Canadian citizens over 18
   - D) citizens who have lived outside Canada for less than five years

8. Polling stations close _____.
   - A) at 8 p.m.
   - B) at 6 p.m.
   - C) at 10 p.m.
   - D) whenever everyone on the voters' list has voted

9. The candidate who wins the most votes in a federal riding becomes
   A) an MLA   B) an MP
   C) a Senator   D) a Cabinet Minister

10. The person who wins the most votes in a provincial riding becomes:
    A) an MLA   B) an MP
    C) a Senator   D) a Cabinet Minister

11. Which of the following is an appointed position?
    A) enumerators   B) MP
    C) Governor General   D) City Councillor

TRUE / FALSE

Circle T if the statement is true. Circle F if it is false.

1. The Prime Minister can call an election for
   a provincial government.   T / F

2. Canadians under 18 can vote in Canada.   T / F

3. Canadians who work for the Canadian government
   outside of Canada can vote.   T / F

4. Enumerators are people who collect names for the voters' list.   T / F

5. Polling stations are only open until 6 p.m.   T / F

6. A person must belong to a political party to become
   a Member of Parliament.   T / F

7. Every Canadian citizen is eligible to vote.   T / F

8. The person who becomes Prime Minister is the leader of
   the party with the most elected MPs.   T / F

FILL IN THE BLANKS

In the blank, write the word(s) needed to complete the sentence.

1. The Prime Minister calls an election about every _____ years.

2. Municipal elections are called about every _____ years.

3. _____ help make up the voters' list by going from door to

   door asking questions to find out who can vote.

4. The place where Canadians vote is called a _____.

5. A _____ is a list of the candidates and the parties they represent for the riding.

6. Polling stations close at _____.

7. Federal elections are called by the _____.

8. A Member of Parliament who does not represent a party is called a(n) _____.

9. A _____ ensures that voting is done properly.

ORDERING

The various steps in the election process are listed below. Number them in the order in which they occur:

_____ Eligible voters receive a notice of enumeration card in the mail.

_____ The voter goes to a polling booth and votes.

_____ The votes are counted.

_____ The ballot is put into a locked box.

_____ The winners of the election are announced.

_____ Voters go the polling station to vote.

_____ The voter's name is crossed off the list and the voter is given a ballot.

_____ The government hires enumerators to count eligible voters.

_____ Enumerators go from door to door and count voters.

_____ The Prime Minister calls an election.

SHORT ANSWER

Answer the following questions.

1. What does representative democracy mean?

2. What is a voters' list?

3. What is a riding or a constituency?

4. What is the role of enumerators in the election process?

5. How can Canadian voters find out about the ideas of the different parties?

6. What is the role of a poll clerk on election day?

7. What does it mean when we say that voting in Canada is done by "secret ballot"?

8. What is the role of scrutineers on election day?

9. How does someone become a Member of Parliament?

10. Name four federal parties in Canada.

Chapter 10 Who Are These Canadians?

MATERIALS REQUIRED *The Canadian Encyclopedia*, a camera.

SKILLS EMPHASIZED Reading comprehension, discussion, identifying, surveying, comparing and contrasting, descriptive writing, role play.

PRE-READING

- ❧ How many famous Canadians can you name?
- ❧ Have you ever heard of Terry Fox?
- ❧ Have you heard of the Marathon of Hope?

READING: TERRY FOX

1 Terry Fox was a young man from British Columbia who discovered he had cancer when he was 19 years old. The doctors had to amputate one of his legs. Terry wanted to do something for other people who had cancer. He planned to run all the way across Canada to raise money for cancer research. In 1980 he began the Marathon of Hope. He started in St. John's, Newfoundland, and was headed for Victoria, BC. Terry ran about 40 kilometres a day. He had to stop near Thunder Bay, Ontario, when his cancer returned. Terry died of lung cancer in 1981.

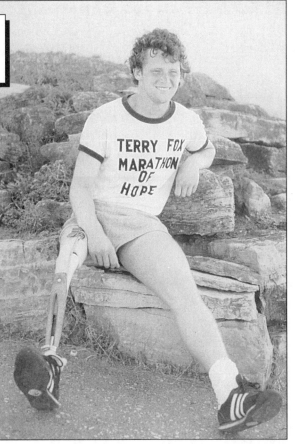

Terry Fox during the Marathon of Hope

Government of Canada

2   Terry Fox has become a hero to all Canadians for his courage and strength. Each year a Terry Fox run is held in most cities in Canada to raise money for cancer research. People who enter the run each year get their friends and families to pay a certain amount of money for every kilometre they complete. This is called sponsoring a runner. They try to get as many people as possible to sponsor the run.

COMPREHENSION AND DISCUSSION QUESTIONS

1. Who was Terry Fox?
2. Why did he plan to run across Canada?
3. How far did he run before he had to stop?
4. Have you ever participated in a fundraising event?
5. Do you know where the marathon originated?
6. Why do you think that Canadians see Terry Fox as a hero?

FAMOUS CANADIANS

Emily Murphy was a popular writer from Alberta. She fought for women's rights in Canada. In 1929, Emily Murphy was responsible for having women declared as "persons" under the law.

Provincial Archives of Alberta

National Archives of Canada

Dr. Frederick Banting and **Dr. Charles Best** were two scientists. In 1922, they discovered insulin. Insulin is given to people with diabetes. Banting and Best's discovery has helped to save the lives of people all over the world.

Government of Canada

In 1984, **Madame Jeanne Sauvé** became the first woman Governor General of Canada.

City of Vancouver Archives; Photographer: Malcolm Perry

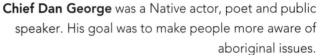

Chief Dan George was a Native actor, poet and public speaker. His goal was to make people more aware of aboriginal issues.

Machal Schmidt Artists International, Inc.

Angela Cheng is a concert pianist who is famous all over the world.

National Archives of Canada

Pauline Johnson was a popular Métis author. She travelled across the country in the early 1900s to read her poetry. She wrote about the Mohawk culture.

FAMOUS CANADIANS

National Archives of Canada

Dr. Norman Bethune was a Canadian surgeon who helped the Spanish and Chinese during their civil wars. Dr. Bethune is a hero to the Chinese people.

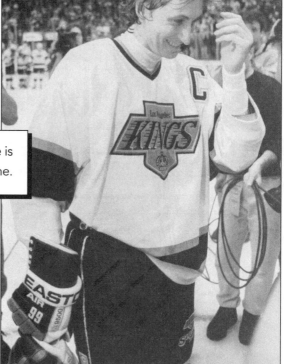

Provincial Archives of Alberta

Wayne Gretzky is also known as "The Great One." He is considered by many to be the finest hockey player of all time.

Government of Canada

In 1984, **Marc Garneau,** a scientist and engineer, was the first Canadian astronaut to go into space.

LANGUAGE AND CONTACT ACTIVITIES

1. More famous Canadians

Using a chart like the one here, ask five Canadians to give you a name of a famous Canadian in each of the categories listed:

Athletes	Writers	Musicians	Artists	Scientists	Political Figures	Actors

Once everyone in class has collected the names, compare your charts.

🐛 Have you heard of any of these people before?

🐛 Whose name appears most often in each of the categories?

🐛 Why are these people famous?

🐛 Were there any categories where some people could not think of a famous Canadian?

2. Who Am I?

Choose one of the names on the chart. Find out as much as you can about this person by a) looking up the name in *The Canadian Encyclopedia*, b) asking your teacher, c) asking other Canadians.

Take on the identity of the person you have chosen. Sit at the front of the class. Your classmates will ask you questions about your identity, such as "when were you born," "why are you famous," etc. They have to ask enough questions so that they can guess who you are. They have three minutes to guess.

3. Name the Most Famous Person

Who is the most famous person in the world (living or dead) in each of the categories listed on the next page.

cowboy	architect
engineer	singer or group of singers
movie star	artist
athlete	royal person
political figure	criminal
warrior	doctor
humanitarian	scientist
religious figure	

4. What do You Know About These Canadians?

In groups, go through the list and see how many of these names you recognize:

Donnacona	Tecumseh	Margaret Atwood
Bryan Adams	Anne Murray	Buffy Sainte Marie
Marshall McLuhan	Gilles Vigneault	Group of Seven
Emily Carr	Pierre Trudeau	Elvis Stojko
Roberta Bondar	Pierre Berton	The Dionne Quintuplets

5. Write a Biography About a Famous Person

Write a short biography about a famous person from your country of origin and share it with the rest of the class. Be sure to include the following information:

🍐 name

🍐 sex

🍐 when the person became famous

🍐 why the person is famous

6. Some Canadian Perspectives

Read the following stories. These people are all Canadians; one was born here, one moved here as a child and the others all chose to come here as adults. These people were asked questions about their perspectives on Canada in interviews. Here are their stories:

Farah Ali Mohamoud is a young mother from Somalia who moved to Canada in 1991. Farah is married to another Somalian; they have one daughter, Jamina, who is two-and-a-half years old. Farah and her husband were married in Saudi Arabia; they decided to move to North America, but Farah said she would not live in the United States. She wanted to come to Canada because it is safer here. She has been

Farah Ali Mohamoud and her daughter

Kelly Robart

studying ESL and plans to go to college this fall. When asked what she likes the most about Canada, Farah said "Canada is a wonderful country; I am very grateful for the chance to bring up my daughter in peace. People can build their lives here." Farah finds the winters in Canada difficult. She was also surprised that many young people are rude and disrespectful. When Farah was asked about the immigration policy, she said that she thinks that people who want to improve their lives should be admitted. She also said that there should be careful screening to ensure that people who start wars or who are criminals are not allowed in.

Leland Gladue is a Cree who spent his first six years on a reserve, but then moved to Edmonton to go to school. Leland had a very hard time in school; when he was growing up, Native children were treated very poorly. He thinks Multiculturalism is good because it helps people to accept different cultural values. Leland says that this openness is good for all Canadians, including Natives. The more diversity, the better it is for the country. Leland likes to see newcomers keep their language and customs. He used to work in the Immigration Department. Although most immigrants want to find jobs and give something back to Canada, Leland says that some people come to this country and expect or demand handouts. This upsets him. He wishes though, that there had been more diversity in the past; that way there may have been greater understanding of Native values. Leland now works at a Canada Employment Centre helping others find jobs.

Leland Gladue

Kelly Robart

Kelly Robart

Lai Nguyen and his children

Lai Nguyen came to Canada from a Thai refugee camp in 1979. Lai was born in Viet Nam and spent his early years working in the family business. In 1977, he was sent by the Army into Cambodia to fight. He was appalled by all the death he saw there. Lai fled Cambodia and went back to Viet Nam where he spent the next two years in hiding. His family convinced him to leave Viet Nam because they were sure he would be found and killed. Lai left for Thailand on a crowded boat. The boat had engine problems, so a three-day trip took eight days. Several people died on the boat. Shortly after his stay in the refugee camp, Lai came to Canada, met and married a Vietnamese woman, and together they had three daughters. After working for several years, Lai started ESL classes. He said that he could understand English fairly well, but now he is learning how to speak well too. When asked why he likes Canada, Lai said that freedom is very important to him. He also likes the standard of living; it's a good place to raise his children. The only thing he doesn't like is the changeable weather. Lai is very worried about other people in war-torn or very poor countries. He thinks Canada should continue to help people through its refugee policy.

Kelly Robart

Gretchen Hess

Gretchen Hess was an American woman who married a Canadian man living in the United States. When her husband decided to return to Canada, Gretchen was quite excited. This was the time of the Viet Nam war (when the US was fighting in Viet Nam). Gretchen and her husband thought that Canada would be a better place to live; they were against the war and wanted to leave the political situation in the USA. First they moved to Winnipeg in the middle of winter. Gretchen was a bit shocked by the cold weather, but she soon got used to it. As soon as she could, Gretchen took out Canadian citizenship. To learn more about Canada, she took courses in Canadian government and politics at a university. Gretchen is now a professor in Educational Psychology. In her job she travels to conferences all over the world. Gretchen says that she is always happy to come back to Canada, her chosen home. Gretchen thinks that Canada is strong because people are proud of their heritage, and diversity is welcome.

Write your story, answering the following questions:

- When did you come here?
- Why did you come?
- What do you like most about Canada?
- What do you like least?
- What makes Canada unique?
- What do you think of Canada's immigration policy?

7. Pictures and Autobiographies

Take pictures of everyone in the class. Compile your stories and your pictures into a book.

GLOSSARY OF TERMS

NOUNS

athlete: a person who is good at sports
biography: the written story of another person's life
courage: bravery
marathon: a race over a very long distance

VERBS

to abide by: to obey
to amputate: to cut off

ADJECTIVES

unique: unusual, special, one of a kind
appalled: horrified, very upset
shocked: very surprised

TEST YOURSELF

Who are These Canadians?

MATCHING

Match the name on the left with the description on the right.

A. Terry Fox   _____ A famous Canadian hockey player

B. Emily Murphy   _____ A world famous concert pianist

C. Dr. Frederick Banting   _____ The first Canadian in space

D. Jeanne Sauvé   _____ A young Canadian who wanted to raise money for cancer research

E. Chief Dan George   _____ A Métis author

F. Pauline Johnson   _____ A writer who fought for women's rights in Canada

G. Dr. Norman Bethune   _____ One of two scientists who discovered insulin

H. Marc Garneau   _____ The first woman Governor General

I. Wayne Gretzky   _____ A Native actor, poet and public speaker

J. Angela Cheng   _____ A famous Canadian surgeon

SHORT ANSWER

Answer the following questions.

1. Who was Terry Fox?

_____

2. What is the Terry Fox run?

_____

3. Why was Emily Murphy important to Canadian history?

_____

4. Explain why Dr. Norman Bethune was famous?

_____

5. What did Dr. Frederick Banting and Dr. Charles Best discover?

_____

Chapter 11   *What is Typically Canadian?*

MATERIALS REQUIRED A recipe for a Canadian dish.

SKILLS EMPHASIZED Reading comprehension, discussion, interviewing, identifying paraphrases, comparing and contrasting, reading and giving instructions, expressing an opinion, predicting, graph reading.

PRE-READING

- What did you know about Canada before you came?
- Have you spent a winter in Canada? If yes, how did you cope?
- Have you been to any national parks?
- What wildlife have you seen in Canada?
- When you think of Canada, what symbols do you think of?

READING: A PORTRAIT OF CANADA

1   The climate of Canada affects the people who live here. In many places winter lasts up to six months. Although it can be mild in some parts of Canada, most people go through some bone-chilling weather each winter. The only way to enjoy the cold is to wear many layers of clothing, including hats, scarves, mitts, parkas, and winter boots. The cold winters make many Canadians want to spend as much time as possible outside during the long hot summer days.

A mountain sheep looking over a valley in the Rockies

Provincial Archives of Alberta

Canada is a huge country. Visitors are surprised at the long distances *2*
between cities. Even more surprising is the fact that Canadians will often travel hundreds of kilometres just for a weekend trip.

Canada has many tourists every year. Most of them come to see the wilderness. *3*
Thousands visit the national parks and wildlife areas to see grizzly bears, moose, elk, deer, and mountain sheep. National and provincial parks are areas where hunting and development are strictly controlled. They are safe environments for plants and animals. The parks save nature for future generations of Canadians to enjoy.

Another important feature of Canada is that it is a bilingual country. In 1969 *4*
the Canadian government passed the Official Languages Act. This law says that all Canadians have the right to communicate with the federal government in either English or French. Every year there are more bilingual Canadians. Many schools have English or French language immersion programs that are the best in the world.

Canada is a multicultural country. This means that Canada is made up of people *5*
from many different cultures. A main goal of multiculturalism is to treat all Canadians as different but equal. Canadians value people from everywhere. There are many social programs in Canada that are designed to make sure that everyone has access to education, health care, and shelter. Although Canada has some problems, in 1994 the United Nations named Canada the best country in the world to live in. It is relatively safe and peaceful, and most people have a good standard of living.

BEWARE OF BUGS AND BEARS!

Although people love to spend time outdoors in the summer, they are sometimes driven inside by the bugs — black flies and mosquitoes especially. These biting pests can ruin a beautiful day unless you have lots of insect repellent.

People like to hike and camp in the wilderness but they have to beware of bears. There are bears in most parts of Canada. Bears can be very dangerous when people feed them or leave garbage behind. In the national parks, visitors are told how to keep food away from bears and what to do if they meet a bear.

Provincial Archives of Alberta

Watch out for grizzly bears like this one

COMPREHENSION AND DISCUSSION QUESTIONS

1. What does it mean to say that Canada is a bilingual country?
2. What does it mean to say that Canada is a multicultural country?
3. Were you surprised by the cold when you first came?
4. What sort of clothing do you wear in the winter?
5. Have you seen any wild animals in Canada?
6. How far would you travel for a weekend vacation?

CANADIAN SYMBOLS

The Maple Leaf: The maple leaf has been a symbol of Canada for many years. It was adopted as the symbol for the Canadian flag in 1965.

Government of Canada

Provincial Archives of Alberta

The Beaver: The beaver has been a symbol of Canada since the beginning of the fur trade. There is a beaver on the Canadian nickel (five cent coin).

Government of Canada

Fleur-de-Lys: The fleur-de-lys is a symbol of Quebec. These children are waving the fleur-de-lys flag.

CANADIAN SYMBOLS CONTINUED

RCMP: For many tourists, the RCMP are the major symbol of Canada. The police force began in the 1870s to keep peace in the west. The RCMP plays an important role today as Canada's national police force.

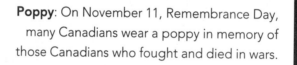

Royal Canadian Mounted Police, RCMP—GRC/87–102–1

Poppy: On November 11, Remembrance Day, many Canadians wear a poppy in memory of those Canadians who fought and died in wars.

Parliament Buildings: Canadians celebrate Confederation on July 1, Canada Day. These Canadians are celebrating on Parliament Hill in Ottawa. Many immigrants become citizens at special ceremonies held on Canada Day.

Government of Canada

Loonie: The Canadian dollar coin is called a loonie because the first time the coin was produced, it had a picture of a loon on one side. The loon is a bird that is found in most parts of Canada. Now, all dollar coins are called loonies, whether they have a picture of a loon on them or not.

Photo Services, University of Alberta

Aboriginal Art: Canadian aboriginal art is prized all over the world.

British Columbia Archives and Records Service

A soapstone carver from Pang, NWT

Government of Canada

Government of Canada

Canadian Coat of Arms: The coat of arms bears Canada's motto, a mari usque ad mare, which is Latin for "from sea to sea."

HOCKEY

Hockey is Canada's national game. The first organized team was started at McGill University in 1879. In 1917, the National Hockey League (NHL) was formed. Over the years new teams have been added to the league but one thing has not changed. Even though many of the cities in the NHL are in the US, most of the best players are Canadian. Every spring, Canadians watch hockey nearly every night to see who the best team in the NHL is. The winning team gets the Stanley Cup. Fans in the city where the winners live celebrate for days. Hockey players make a lot of money. Many children play hockey from an early age, hoping to join the NHL. Hockey has become a very popular sport throughout Europe and North America.

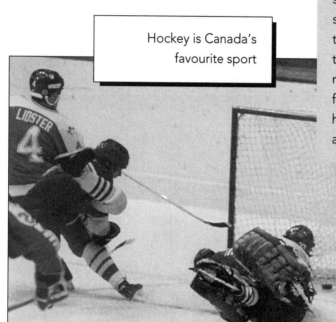

Hockey is Canada's favourite sport

Provincial Archives of Alberta

LANGUAGE AND CONTACT ACTIVITIES

1. Eating Habits

Interview another classmate using the following questions; then write a profile of your classmate's eating habits and views.

- ❧ What is your favourite food?
- ❧ Have your eating habits changed since coming to Canada?
- ❧ Do you cook? What do you like to cook?

- What do you think about vegetarianism?
- Are you allergic to any foods?
- Are there any foods that you won't eat? If so, why not?
- What kind of food do you think is typically Canadian?

2. Recipes

Saskatoons are berries found all over the prairies. They are similar to blueberries, but they are smaller. Here is a recipe for Saskatoon Berry Pie. Read it carefully. Some of the instructions are not necessary and others are very important. Your friend has asked you for a short and easy recipe. Cross out the unnecessary instructions.

CANADIAN CUISINE

The cooking styles in Canada have come from all over the world. There are restaurants which serve the specialties of dozens of different countries. Although there are few truly Canadian dishes, regions of Canada are well known for some of the food they produce. On the West Coast people enjoy seafood, particularly salmon and crab. The East Coast is known for its lobster and cod. Alberta is famous for its beef. Prairie wheat makes the finest pasta and bread. The fruit from the Okanagan region of British Columbia and Southern Ontario is transported all over the rest of the country. Wonderful berries are grown nearly everywhere in Canada. Quebec maintains French cuisine, and specialties include tortiere (a meat pie), soups, and maple syrup. Wild rice is a delicacy found in Manitoba and Ontario. In the North, lake fish (such as trout and Arctic char) are very popular.

SASKATOON BERRY PIE

Frozen pie shell

4 cups of fresh Saskatoon berries (you can substitute blueberries if you do not have Saskatoons)

1 cup of sugar

4 tablespoons flour

2 teaspoons cornstarch

1 1/2 tablespoons lemon juice

1/2 teaspoon cinnamon

1 tablespoon butter

Line a 9 inch pan with a pie shell or pie crust; that is put the pie crust inside a 9 inch pie pan.

Clean the berries. Wash them carefully, make sure to get all little twigs off them. Don't bruise the berries.

Continued on the next page

Continued from page 139

Combine the sugar, flour, cornstarch, lemon juice, and cinnamon. Put all these ingredients in one bowl and stir them together.

Mix the contents of the bowl with the berries. Sprinkle these ingredients over the berries and stir them gently until they are well blended.

Pour the mixture into the pie crust.

Dot the berries with butter; that is, take little bits of butter and put them all over the top of the berries.

Let the pie sit for 15 minutes. Then cover the berries with a top crust. If you like you can use a fork to make a pretty pattern in the pastry, but it is not necessary.

Make sure the oven is at 450°. Bake the pie at 450° for 10 minutes. Lower the heat to 350°. Bake the pie for another 30 minutes or until the crust is brown.

Write down your favourite recipe. Share it with the class. Together, plan a pot luck party, where everyone cooks a dish and brings it to share with everyone else.

3. Your Impressions of Canada

List your first impressions of Canada.

- What surprised you the most?
- What did you like the most?
- What did you dislike the most?
- Today, how do you feel about your first impressions? How have they changed?
- What do you like about living in Canada today?
- What do you dislike about living here?

4. Typical Symbols

Ask five Canadians to tell you what symbols they think are typically Canadian. Compare the answers you've collected with those of your classmates.

- Which symbols were mentioned most often?
- Were there any answers that surprised you?

What are typical symbols from your country?

5. Hours of Daylight in Windsor and Inuvik

Locate Windsor, Ontario on a map.

This line graph shows the average number of hours of daylight each month for Windsor. Look at the graph and answer the following questions.

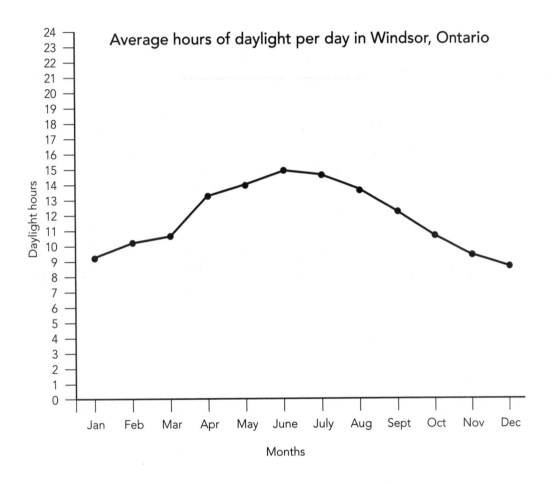

- ❧ Which month had the most daylight?
- ❧ Which month had the least daylight?
- ❧ What was the average number of hours of daylight in December? in June? in September?
- ❧ What was the average number of hours of daylight for the whole year?

The graph on the following page is called a bar graph. It shows exactly the same information as the line graph.

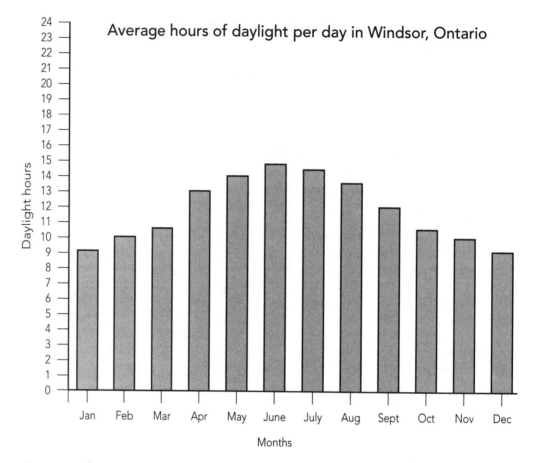

Average hours of daylight per day in Windsor, Ontario

Compare the two graphs.

🐛 Which one do you find easier to read? Why?

🐛 Put a piece of blank paper on top of the line graph. Make a dot on the top of each bar. Join the dots together with lines.

🐛 Compare your drawing with the line graph. Are they the same?

Locate Inuvik on a map. The following are the average number of hours and minutes of daylight for each month in Inuvik:

Month	Hours & Minutes	Month	Hours & Minutes
January	3:08	July	22:01
February	7:41	August	17:35
March	11:41	September	13:15
April	16:16	October	9:10
May	21:05	November	3:50
June	24:00	December	00:21

Put the average number of daylight hours for each month in Inuvik on the graph below. Then make a line or bar graph.

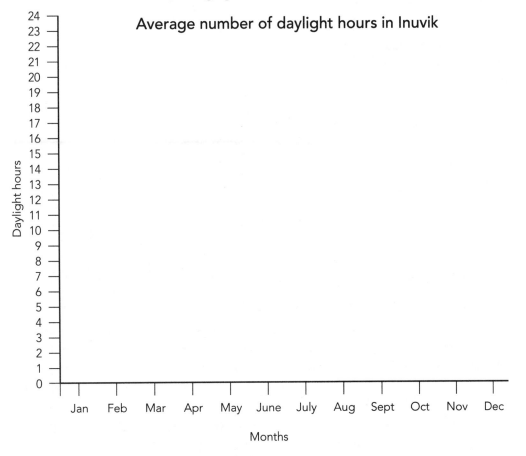

Average number of daylight hours in Inuvik

🐾 Which month had the most daylight?

🐾 Which month had the least daylight?

🐾 What was the average number of hours of daylight in December? In June? In September?

🐾 What was the average number of hours of daylight for the whole year?

Compare the graph of Inuvik to the graph of Windsor.

🐾 Are there any months that had nearly the same amount of daylight in both places?

🐾 In Windsor, the number of hours of daylight ranges from a high of 15 hours and 15 minutes in June to a low of 9 hours in December. What is the range in Inuvik?

🐾 Which place would you rather live?

In Inuvik, there are 55 days in the summer that have 24 hours of sunlight. The sun never rises or sets on these days. In the winter there are 30 days when there is no sunlight at all. The sun neither rises nor sets. On how many days of the year in Inuvik does the sun rise and set?

GUN CONTROL

Although there are many similarities between Canada and the USA, one striking difference is people's attitudes towards guns. While Americans protect their right to bear arms, most Canadians are proud to have strict gun control laws. In fact, some Canadians would like to ban all guns. The result of the gun control laws in Canada is that Canadians have much higher levels of personal safety. The number of deaths by guns in the USA is extremely high, while it is quite rare for Canadians to be shot to death.

6. Gun Control

In pairs, write down as many arguments as you can in two columns: for and against gun control. Would you ever want to own a gun? Why or why not?

THE CANADIAN IDENTITY: IS THERE ONE?

Every year around July first, newspaper and magazine columnists ask the question, "What does it mean to be a Canadian?" They never seem to come to a definite answer. Canadians have been described as both friendly and cold, outgoing and reserved, boring and mysterious. How is it that Canadians can be all these things at once? Canada is a nation of immigrants from all over the world. Every time a new group of people makes its home here, the country changes a little more. The beliefs and opinions of one group will often be very different from those of another.

Canadians think peace is important, so they usually try to accommodate each other. The way in which Canadians adapt to change is through compromise, or finding a middle ground. Some people see compromise, understanding, acceptance of difference, and a desire for peace as the essential components of the Canadian identity. Others say that these attributes only suggest that Canadians do not share a common set of values and that there is no Canadian identity.

FOLLOW-UP

- ❧ What is your impression of Canadian people?
- ❧ How would you describe the Canadian identity?
- ❧ How do you deal with people who have different beliefs and values from your own?

🐦 Some immigrants comment that Canadian children have too much freedom and that they are badly behaved. They say that there is a need for more discipline. What do you think?

🐦 Some newcomers say that although Canadians smile and seem friendly, they don't really welcome immigrants. Some people say that they would prefer open discrimination to the polite discrimination in Canada. What do you think about this?

🐦 What do you think the Canadian identity will be in twenty years?

GLOSSARY OF TERMS

NOUNS

component: part

cuisine: cooking

immersion program: a method of teaching a second language by teaching content through the new language

insect repellent: chemical used to keep insects from biting

parka: winter jacket

pest: an annoying insect

right to bear arms: the right to carry guns

vegetarianism: the practice of not eating meat

wilderness: an area of land with no development

wildlife: plants and animals in the wild

VERBS

to accommodate: to make room for; to adjust

to adapt: to adjust

to ban: to forbid the use of

ADJECTIVES

allergic: suffering from a reaction to a substance

boring: not interesting

essential: necessary

mysterious: not easy to understand

obvious: clear

reserved: hiding feelings

striking: noticeable

⬛ TEST YOURSELF ⬛

What is Typically Canadian?

TRUE / FALSE

Circle T if the statement is true. Circle F if it is false.

1. Canada has very long summers.   T / F

2. Canada has very long winters.   T / F

3. The maple leaf was adopted as the symbol for the
    Canadian flag in 1965.   T / F

4. The beaver as a symbol of Canada originated from
    the fur trade.   T / F

5. The fleur-de-lys is a symbol for the province of Nova Scotia.   T / F

6. The poppy symbolizes Thanksgiving.   T / F

7. The days in winter are short.   T / F

8. Jasper is a national park.   T / F

9. Canada is a multicultural country   T / F

FILL IN THE BLANKS

In the blank, write the word(s) needed to make the sentence complete.

1. The two official languages in Canada are _____ and

    _____ .

2. The fleur-de-lys is a symbol for the province of _____.

3. The symbol used to commemorate Remembrance Day is the

    _____.

4. The _____ was adopted as the symbol for the Canadian
   flag in 1965.

5. _____ is the most popular sport in Canada.

MATCHING

Match the Canadian symbols on the left with the description on the right.

A. Maple Leaf   _____ "a mari usque ad mare"

B. Beaver   _____ Canada's national police force

C. Fleur-de-lys   _____ symbol on the Canadian flag

D. Poppy   _____ symbol on the nickel

E. RCMP   _____ nickname for the Canadian dollar

F. Parliament Buildings   _____ symbol on the Quebec flag

G. Loonie   _____ symbol of Remembrance Day

H. Motto on the Coat of Arms   _____ located in Ottawa

SHORT ANSWER

Answer the following questions.

1. What is a national park?

_____

2. What does it mean when people refer to Canada as a bilingual country?

_____

3. What does it mean when people refer to Canada as a multicultural country?

_____

4. Why do Canadians call their dollar coin a loonie?

_____

5. What is a goal of multiculturalism?

_____

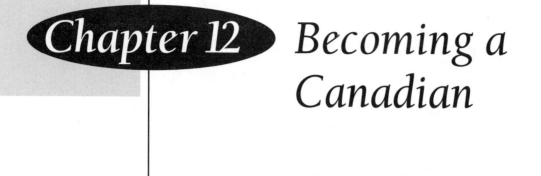

Chapter 12 · Becoming a Canadian

MATERIALS REQUIRED The Charter of Rights and Freedoms, sample citizenship application forms, Oath of Canadian Citizenship.

SKILLS EMPHASIZED Reading comprehension, discussion, comparing and contrasting, problem-solving, listing, letter writing, expressing opinions.

PRE-READING I

- ❧ Why do you think most people come to Canada?
- ❧ Have you heard of the Charter of Rights and Freedoms?
- ❧ What basic rights do you think all human beings should have?

READING I: CANADIAN RIGHTS AND RESPONSIBILITIES

1 Many people come to Canada because they want to be free. Canadians have more freedom than people in many other countries in the world. The Charter of Rights and Freedoms is the law that gives Canadians their freedom. It is part of the Constitution, which is the most important law in Canada.

2 What kinds of freedoms do Canadians have?

- ❧ Freedom of religion — people can follow any religion. There are Christians, Jews, Moslems, Buddhists, Hindus, and people of other religions in Canada. There are also people who have no religion.

🍎 Freedom of thought, belief, opinion and expression, including freedom of the press. This means that Canadians can say what they think and news media can print stories that might not get printed in other countries. For example, if a Canadian doesn't like a politician, he or she is free to say so.

🍎 Freedom of peaceful assembly. This means that a group of people can meet. In some countries, groups are not allowed to hold meetings.

Canadians also have basic rights.   3

🍎 Canadians have the right to vote in elections.

🍎 Canadians have the right to live and work anywhere in Canada.

🍎 Canadians have the right to run in an election.

🍎 Canadians have the right to be treated equally regardless of their sex, race, colour, national or ethnic origin, age, mental or physical disability.

🍎 Canadians have legal rights. They cannot be arrested without an explanation. Their property cannot be searched or taken away without explanation.

The following responsibilities go along with the rights.   4

🍎 to vote in elections

🍎 to be loyal to Canada

🍎 to learn and obey the laws of the country

🍎 to refrain from discrimination against others

🍎 to participate in the community

🍎 to care for Canada's heritage

For Canada to function well as a society, it is important for all Canadians to take   5
their rights and responsibilities seriously.

COMPREHENSION AND DISCUSSION QUESTIONS:

1. Name three freedoms that Canadians enjoy.

2. Name four rights.

3. Are there any rights that Canadians have that you didn't have in the country that you came from? Are there any rights that people in your former country have that Canadians don't have?

4. What do you think it means to be loyal to Canada?

5. Are there any laws in Canada that are different from the laws in your former country?

6. What are some ways in which you can participate in the community?

LANGUAGE AND CONTACT ACTIVITIES

1. Responsibilities of Canadian citizens

List the responsibilities of Canadian citizens and give an example of each one. For example:

RESPONSIBILITY	EXAMPLE
Care for Canada's heritage	Don't litter

2. Problem-solving

In pairs or groups discuss how you would handle the following situations involving rights and responsibilities:

- 🍃 Your drunken neighbour makes loud noise all night long.

- 🍃 Your child comes home from school and tells you that children were calling her nasty names.

- 🍃 Your Chinese friend phones to see an apartment. As soon as the landlord sees that he is Chinese, he says the apartment has been rented. You find out later that the apartment hadn't been rented.

- 🍃 You look out the window and see someone breaking into the house across the street.

- 🍃 You are working a lot of overtime and you are not getting paid for it. Your boss says that he just can't afford it.

Can you think of some difficult situations where people's rights have been violated or where other people have not met their responsibility?

3. Volunteering

Find out if there is a central volunteer bureau in your community. Write to the bureau for information on the types of volunteer jobs available. If there is no central volunteer bureau, contact the United Way and ask for someone to come to your class to talk to you about volunteer opportunities.

FOLLOW-UP

- Do you do any volunteer work?
- Some people have criticized the existence of food banks. They say that the government has the responsibility to provide for the needs of disadvantaged people. They say that as long as food banks exist, the government will not meet its responsibility. What do you think?
- The federal government spends a lot of money providing language classes for newcomers. The purpose of this spending is to help immigrants become active participants in the Canadian community. Do you think it works? What do you think would be the best way to help immigrants participate in the community?

THE ROLE OF COMMUNITY

One of the responsibilities of Canadians is to participate in the community. When Europeans first came, the aboriginal people helped them to survive. Each group of immigrants faces difficult situations. Without the support of people in their communities it would be even harder for newcomers. Today, participation in the community can mean many different things. There are many social problems which are partly addressed by volunteers. For example, every large city in Canada has food banks. People donate food and hours of work to help others who do not have enough food. Canadians volunteer to help at community celebrations, in ESL programs, at hospitals, churches and at many social service agencies. People coach children in sports and help out at schools. There are many different ways to participate in a community.

PRE-READING II

- Do you know anyone who has recently become a Canadian?
- Are you planning to become a Canadian citizen?
- What does it mean to be a Canadian?
- What steps do you have to go through to become a Canadian?

READING II: APPLYING FOR CANADIAN CITIZENSHIP

Chunhui and Ming Ming Cheung came to Canada three years ago with their two children, Sue (age 6) and Victor (age 9). They started a small cleaning business that is

1

doing very well. Although the first year was difficult for the Cheungs, they gradually started to feel comfortable in Canada. When they had been here for three years, they decided to become Canadian citizens.

2   Ming Ming phoned the office of Canadian citizenship to find out what the Cheungs needed to do. She was surprised to hear a telephone answering machine. She listened once, then hung up and called back so that she could hear the message again. The message gave the address of the citizenship office. Ming Ming wrote it down, and a couple of days later she went there to pick up citizenship application forms for the whole family. When she brought the forms home, everyone looked them over. They made a list of all the documents they would need to bring to their appointment with a citizenship officer and they filled out the applications.

3   On the day that the Cheungs took in their applications, they met with a citizenship officer. The officer looked through all their documents and the application forms to make sure that everything was in order. She gave the Cheungs some study materials to help them prepare for the citizenship test. She told them that they would be notified of the time, day, and place of the test. She also told them that the children did not need to take the test.

4   The Cheungs went home and looked at the study materials. Ming Ming was quite worried that she wouldn't be able to pass the test. She called her friend Ella and asked her what to do. Ella had just recently received Canadian citizenship. Ella told Ming Ming not to worry. She told her about the citizenship course she had taken. The course helped Ella to understand Canadian geography, history, government, elections, and rights and responsibilities. Ella said that she felt confident when she took the test because the course had covered all of those areas.

5   Ming Ming told Chunhui about the classes. Chunhui told his wife that she could take the classes but that he would rather study on his own. They could then practise testing each other.

6   Finally the day of the test came. Both Chunhui and Ming Ming were very nervous. They took the test. Both of them passed. Their studying was successful.

7   The last and most enjoyable step for the Cheungs was the citizenship ceremony. Everyone dressed up in their best clothes. When they got to the hall, the children were excited to see a Mountie in the red uniform. There were many other people getting their citizenship too. First, there was a speech by a prominent Canadian who later awarded citizenship to all the new Canadians. The Cheungs felt very proud as they repeated the oath of Canadian citizenship. Ming Ming had tears in her eyes. There was a reception after the ceremony. Then the whole family went out for dinner to celebrate their new country.

COMPREHENSION AND DISCUSSION QUESTIONS

1. How many years were the Cheungs in Canada before they decided to become Canadian citizens?

2. What steps are involved in becoming a Canadian?

3. What do people have to know to pass the citizenship test?

4. Do you think that most people who are born in Canada would pass the citizenship test?

5. Do you think it is important for Canadians to know about geography? history? government? elections? rights and responsibilities? Explain your answers.

LANGUAGE AND CONTACT ACTIVITIES

1. The Citizenship Application Form

Get a citizenship application form from your teacher or from the citizenship office. Answer the following questions.

- What documents must be provided with your application?
- Can you use passport photos?
- Can you apply for more than one person on a single form?
- Which of the following information is not required?

   a) marital status

   b) birthdate

   c) date of entry to Canada

   d) place of work

- Why do you think the government wants to know whether an applicant has committed a crime? Do you think that someone who has committed a crime should be allowed to become a citizen?

2. The Citizenship Ceremony

Choose one student to phone the citizenship office in your community. The student should ask where and when the next citizenship ceremony will be held. Arrange as a class to go to the ceremony. After the ceremony, talk to some of the new Canadians. Ask them how they feel.

3. Test Each Other

Make up five questions that you think new Canadians should be able to answer. Put your questions on strips of paper and place them in an envelope. Divide the class into two teams, A and B. One person from Team A chooses a question from the envelope to ask a person in Team B. If the person gets the right answer, Team B gets a point. Play until everyone on both teams has had a turn. The team with the most points is the winner.

GLOSSARY OF TERMS

NOUNS

bureau: office
ceremony: formal celebration
documents: legal papers
heritage: background, personal cultural history
mountie: RCMP officer
oath: sacred promise
reception: party, gathering

VERBS

to coach: to teach
to criticize: to find fault
to donate: to give
to litter: to drop garbage on the ground
to notify: to tell
to refrain: to stop, to keep from doing something
to violate: to show disrespect
to volunteer: to give of one's time, to work for no pay

ADJECTIVES

confident: sure, secure, self-assured, positive
nasty: mean, cruel
prominent: important

ADVERBS

gradually: slowly

TEST YOURSELF

Becoming a Canadian

MULTIPLE CHOICE

Circle the best answer.

1. Which of the following is not a freedom of Canadians?
   a) the freedom to steal
   b) the freedom of religion
   c) the freedom of the press
   d) the freedom of assembly

2. Canadians have the basic right to _____.
   a) take Sundays off from work
   b) take the law into their own hands
   c) run in an election
   d) discriminate against others

3. Which of the following is not a basic right of Canadians?
   a) the right to run in an election
   b) the right to be treated equally
   c) the right to vote in elections
   d) the right to bear arms

4. Which of the following is not a responsibility of Canadians?
   a) to participate in the community
   b) to accept government's decisions
   c) to vote in elections
   d) to be loyal to Canada

5. Along with their rights, Canadians are responsible to _____.
   a) make sure others follow the laws of Canada
   b) treat other cultural groups differently
   c) support political candidates even if they do not like them
   d) care for Canada's heritage

6. An example of voluntary work is _____.
   a) a job that pays equal to or less than minimum wage
   b) cleaning your house on the weekend
   c) donating your time and effort to a cause
   d) doing work you don't like

TRUE / FALSE

Circle T if the statement is true. Circle F if it is false.

1. Canadians have less freedom than people in most other countries. T / F

2. A Canadian does not have the right to express dissatisfaction
   with the government.   T / F

3. Canadians have the freedom the follow any religion they wish.   T / F

4. Canadians do not have the freedom to meet in groups.   T / F

5. Canadians have the right to vote in elections.   T / F

6. Canadians are not free to live and work anywhere in Canada.   T / F

7. Canadians should be loyal to Canada.   T / F

FILL IN THE BLANKS

In the blank, write the word(s) needed to make the sentence complete.

1. Being able to go to any church or any temple is an example of

   _____.

2. Canadians have _____ freedom than people in many other

   countries.

3. Learning and obeying the laws of Canada are _____.

4. _____ is the law that ensures Canadians' freedom.

5. To be treated equally in Canada is a _____.

6. Teaching literacy classes on Saturday mornings without being paid is an

   example of _____.

SHORT ANSWER

Answer the following questions.

1. Identify three freedoms of Canadians.

2. Identify four basics rights of Canadians.

   _____

3. Identify five responsibilities of Canadians.

   _____

4. What does it mean when we say that Canadians have freedom of the press?

   _____

5. Why do you want to become a Canadian?

   _____

Chapter 13 Citizenship Practice Test

Circle the best answer.

1. Canada has _____.
   A) eight provinces
   B) ten provinces
   C) three territories
   D) one territory

2. The capital of Canada is _____.
   A) Toronto
   B) Ottawa
   C) Montreal
   D) Vancouver

3. Who were the first people to come to Canada?
   A) the English
   B) the French
   C) the Indians
   D) the Americans

4. Quebec City was built by _____.
   A) Sir Wilfrid Laurier
   B) Samuel de Champlain
   C) Jacques Cartier
   D) John Cabot

5. Which was the last province to join Confederation?
   A) Alberta
   B) Saskatchewan
   C) Newfoundland
   D) Nova Scotia

6. Which province did not sign the Constitution Act, 1982?
   A) Quebec
   B) Newfoundland
   C) Manitoba
   D) British Columbia

7. Who was the first Prime Minister of Canada?
   A) Sir John A. Macdonald
   B) Wilfrid Laurier
   C) Pierre Elliott Trudeau
   D) Mackenzie King

8. The Queen's representative in the federal government is
   A) the Prime Minister
   B) the Lieutenant Governor
   C) the Governor General
   D) the Mayor

9. The three levels of government in Canada are

   A) federal, provincial, national
   B) federal, Senate, civil
   C) local, provincial, municipal
   D) federal, provincial, municipal

10. The Prime Minister of Canada is
    A) the person who receives the most votes
    B) the leader of the party with the most elected MPs
    C) the leader of the party that gets the most votes
    D) appointed by the House of Commons

11. The federal Parliament is made up of
    A) the House of Commons and the Senate
    B) Governor General, Prime Minister
    C) government and official opposition
    D) Prime Minister and Cabinet

12. Who calls an election in Canada?
    A) the Prime Minister
    B) the Governor General
    C) the Queen
    D) the MPs

13. All of the following people are eligible to vote in Canada except
    A) citizens outside Canada who work for the government
    B) Canadian citizens over 18 years of age
    C) Canadian citizens under 18
    D) Canadian citizens who have lived outside Canada for less than five years

14. The candidate who wins the most votes in a federal riding becomes
    A) an MLA
    B) an MP
    C) a Senator
    D) a Cabinet Minister

15. A majority government
    A) is elected every four years
    B) has fewer seats than the official opposition
    C) has the same number of seats as the official opposition
    D) has more seats than all the opposition parties combined

16. What do enumerators count?
    A) candidates
    B) voters
    C) MPs
    D) MLAs

17. Which of the following is not a freedom of Canadians?
    A) the freedom to steal
    B) the freedom of religion
    C) the freedom of speech
    D) the freedom of assembly

18. Canadians have the basic right to
    A) take Sundays off from work
    B) take the law into their own hands
    C) run in an election
    D) discriminate against others

19. Which of the following is not a basic right of Canadians?
    A) the right to run in an election
    B) the right to be treated equally
    C) the right to vote in elections
    D) the right to bear arms

20. Which of the following is not a responsibility of Canadians?
    A) to participate in the community
    B) to accept the government's decisions
    C) to vote in elections
    D) to be loyal to Canada

21. Which political party is the official opposition in the federal parliament?
    A) Progressive Conservative Party
    B) Liberal Party of Canada
    C) Bloc Quebecois
    D) Reform Party of Canada
    E) New Democratic Party
    F) other

ANSWER KEY

1. B
2. B
3. C
4. B
5. C
6. A
7. A
8. C
9. D
10. B
11. A

12. A
13. C
14. B
15. D
16. B
17. A
18. C
19. D
20. B
21. Ask your teacher

Test Yourself Answer Keys

Chapter 1: What Does Canada Look Like?

MULTIPLE CHOICE

1. B	4. C	7. D
2. B	5. A	8. C
3. B	6. B	9. A

TRUE / FALSE

1. F	4. F	7. F	10. T
2. F	5. T	8. T	11. T
3. F	6. T	9. F	

FILL IN THE BLANKS

1. 27
2. Whitehorse
3. United States
4. Regina
5. Newfoundland
6. Toronto
7. English, French
8. 10, 2
9. Victoria
10. Pacific, Atlantic, Arctic

MATCHING

K Yellowknife	C Regina
G Fredericton	D Winnipeg
B Edmonton	A Victoria
I Charlottetown	H Halifax
L Whitehorse	F Quebec City
E Toronto	J St. John's

SHORT ANSWER

1. The Atlantic, Pacific and Arctic oceans surround Canada.

2. The last province to join Confederation was Newfoundland.

3. The Great Lakes are: Lake Superior, Lake Michigan, Lake Huron, Lake Erie, and Lake Ontario.

4. The prairie provinces are Alberta, Saskatchewan and Manitoba.

5. A Chinook is a warm wind that blows over the mountains on to the prairies.

6. The new territory will be called Nunavut.

7. The three R's stand for Reduce, Reuse, and Recycle.

8. The four Atlantic provinces are Nova Scotia, New Brunswick, Newfoundland and PEI

9. The main industries of the prairie provinces are: farming, oil & gas, cattle, mining, hydroelectricity, and tourism.

10. The main industries of the Atlantic provinces are forestry, fishing, mining, gas & oil, food processing, farming, and tourism.

Chapter 2: Canada's First Peoples

MULTIPLE CHOICE

1. C   4. B
2. D   5. A
3. B

TRUE / FALSE

1. T   4. T
2. F   5. T
3. F

FILL IN THE BLANKS

1. Igloos   6. hunting, fishing
2. 30 000   7. hunting (buffalo)
3. 5000   8. farming, hunting
4. 1497   9. reserves
5. 1534

SHORT ANSWER

1. Scientists think that the Indians came to Canada across the Bering Strait.

2. The Europeans brought diseases to the Indians when they first came to Canada.

3. A reserve is land for native use only.

4. Native people value cooperation and respect for the land.

5. Today, native people face discrimination, poor education, alcoholism, and high unemployment.

Chapter 3: Our English and French Heritage

MULTIPLE CHOICE

1. D   4. D
2. D   5. A
3. B   6. C

TRUE / FALSE

1. F   4. F
2. F   5. T
3. F

FILL IN THE BLANKS

1. England, France
2. Quebec
3. Acadians
4. Separate
5. 1980

SHORT ANSWER

1. About 80% of people living in Quebec speak French as their first language.
2. Acadia is made up of Nova Scotia and New Brunswick.
3. Most Acadians moved to Louisiana after being deported from Acadia.
4. The provincial political party that was formed in Quebec in the 1960s was the Parti Quebecois.
5. The federal political party that was recently formed was the Bloc Quebecois.

Chapter 4: Confederation

MULTIPLE CHOICE

1. C   4. C   7. A
2. B   5. B   8. B
3. D   6. A

TRUE / FALSE

1. T   4. T   7. T   10. T
2. F   5. T   8. T   11. F
3. F   6. F   9. T

FILL IN THE BLANKS

1. 1867   6. December 25
2. Confederation   7. January 1
3. Sir John A. Macdonald   8. Manitoba
4. July 1   9. Trudeau
5. November 11

MATCHING

1870   K   D
1867   E   F   G   H
1905   B   C
1873   I
1898   L
1871   A
1949   J

E November 11
I December 26
A July 1
F January 1
B December 25
D February 14
C October 31
G March 17

F citizenship   M recycling
M utilities   F currency
P education   F post office
P highways   F immigration
M garbage collection   F defence
F unemployment insurance   P health care

SHORT ANSWER

1. Ontario, Quebec, Nova Scotia and New Brunswick joined together to become Canada in 1867.

2. The national holiday of Canada is "Canada Day."

3. The British North America Act was Canada's first constitution. It outlined the responsibilities of both the federal and provincial governments.

4. Louis Riel was a Métis who led a rebellion to stop Manitoba from joining Canada.

5. Alberta and Saskatchewan entered into Confederation in 1905.

6. The three levels of government in Canada are federal, provincial and municipal.

7. Federal responsibilities include: citizenship, defence, post office, unemployment insurance, foreign policy, currency, Canada Pension, RCMP, and immigration.

8. Provincial responsibilities include: health care, education, licenses and highways.

9. Municipal responsibilities include: garbage collection, utilities, recycling, water, fire protection, streets, and city police.

Chapter 5: Tying the Nation Together

MULTIPLE CHOICE

1. B   4. C

2. B   5. A

3. C

TRUE / FALSE

1. F   4. T

2. T   5. F

3. F   6. T

MATCHING

G 1991

E 1939

F 1756

C 1869

B 1914

D 1812

A 1950

SHORT ANSWER

1. The government bought land to enlarge the size of the country and to build the Canadian Pacific Railway.

2. John A. Macdonald wanted Canada to stretch from sea to sea.

3. John A. Macdonald wanted to build the Canadian Pacific Railway to unite the country.

4. The Canadian Shield and the Rocky Mountains made it difficult and dangerous to build the Canadian Pacific Railway.

5. The Canadian Pacific Railway was used for travel and transportation of goods (e.g., wheat).

6. Many people moved to Canada from the United States because they were loyal to the King of England.

7. The border between Canada and the United States was established at the end of the war in 1812.

Chapter 6: Canada Today: A Multicultural Society

MULTIPLE CHOICE

1. B   4. D
2. B   5. C
3. D

TRUE / FALSE

1. T   4. T
2. T   5. F
3. F   6. T

FILL IN THE BLANKS

1. 1988
2. mosaic
3. first
4. Non-Europeans

SHORT ANSWER

1. The federal government wanted to settle the west.

2. Points are awarded for occupation, language ability, education, work experience, and financial status.

3. The greatest immigration occurred prior to World War I: 1905-1913.

4. People came to Canada in the late 1800s because they wanted freedom. In addition, many poor people could afford to buy land.

5. Immigrants first came to Canada to begin a better life and to take advantage of the inexpensive land that was offered to them.

Chapter 7: What do Canadians do?

TRUE / FALSE

1. T		5. T
2. F		6. F
3. T		7. F
4. T		8. F

SHORT ANSWER

1. Natural resources in British Columbia are: forests, fish, minerals, and fruit.

2. Industries in Prince Edward Island are: potato farming and tourism.

3. The main industries in Quebec are: manufacturing, hydroelectricity, mining, dairy farming, and tourism.

4. The main industries in Manitoba are: farming and hydroelectricity.

5. The main industries in Ontario are: manufacturing, mining, fruit, and tourism.

6. The main industries in New Brunswick are: forestry and food processing.

7. One of the most important changes in the workplace in Canada is that women have joined the work force.

8. Canadians enjoy swimming, fishing, gardening, bicycling, walking, camping and hiking during the summer.

9. Canadians enjoy skiing, skidooing, skating, hockey, reading, and watching T.V. during the winter.

10. Christianity has the biggest following in Canada.

Chapter 8: How is Canada Governed?

MULTIPLE CHOICE

1. C	4. A	7. D	10. A
2. B	5. B	8. C	11. B
3. A	6. D	9. C	

TRUE / FALSE

1. F	5. F
2. T	6. F
3. F	7. T
4. F	

FILL IN THE BLANKS

1. Ask your teacher
2. three
3. Senate
4. Government
5. Official Opposition
6. Prime Minister
7. Legislative Assembly (legislature)
8. Premier
9. Mayor, Councillors
10. Bill
11. Royal assent

MATCHING

C The Queen's representative in the Provincial government

F Appointed by the Prime Minister

G The leader of the party with the most MLAs elected

A The leader of the party with the most MPs elected

D A person who is elected to the provincial government

B The Queen's representative in the Federal government

E The party with the second most MPs elected

H A person who is elected to the federal government

SHORT ANSWER

1. The Governor General represents the Queen in the federal government.

2. Members of Parliament are elected people in the House of Commons.

3. Members of Parliament are elected by the people.

4. Senators are appointed by the Prime Minister.

5. The Prime Minister is the leader of the party that has the most elected MPs.

6. Cabinet Ministers give advice and help in certain areas of the government, for example, Finance and Defence.

7. The Lieutenant Governor represents the Queen in the provincial government.

8. The Premier is the leader of the party who has the most elected MLAs.

9. A bill is a piece of legislation or a suggestion for a law that is written down.

10. Royal assent occurs when the Governor General signs a bill.

Chapter 9: Elections

MULTIPLE CHOICE

1. A	4. C	7. A	10. A
2. A	5. C	8. A	11. C
3. B	6. D	9. B	

TRUE / FALSE

1. F	4. T	7. F
2. F	5. F	8. T
3. T	6. F	

FILL IN THE BLANKS

1. Five	4. polling station	7. Prime Minister
2. Three	5. ballot	8. Independent
3. Enumerators	6. 8 p.m.	9. Scrutineer

ORDERING

<u>4</u> Eligible voters receive a notice of enumeration card in the mail.

<u>7</u> The voter goes to a polling booth and votes.

<u>9</u> The votes are counted.

<u>8</u> The ballot is put into a locked box.

<u>10</u> The winners of the election are announced.

<u>5</u> Voters go the polling station to vote.

<u>6</u> The voter's name is crossed off the list and the voter is given a ballot.

<u>2</u> The government hires enumerators to count eligible voters.

<u>3</u> Enumerators go from door to door.

<u>1</u> The Prime Minister calls an election.

SHORT ANSWER

1. A representative democracy means that the people elect representatives to make decisions for them.

2. A voters' list is a list of people eligible to vote in an election.

3. A riding or a constituency is a geographical section or area of the country. People who live in the riding choose a candidate to represent them.

4. Enumerators count the number of eligible voters for each riding in Canada.

5. Canadian voters find out about the ideas of the different parties by listening to the radio, watching the television, going to community meetings, talking to friends, reading the newspaper, and reading brochures delivered to them.

6. The role of the poll clerk is to make sure each person who comes to vote is eligible. They also ensure that a person only votes once.

7. A secret ballot means that no one sees who a person votes for.

8. Scrutineers ensure that voting is done properly.

9. A person becomes a Member of Parliament by being elected.

10. The federal parties in Canada include the Liberal party, the Conservative party, the Reform party, the New Democratic party, and the Bloc Quebecois.

Chapter 10: Who are these Canadians?

MATCHING

I   A famous Canadian hockey player

J   A world famous concert pianist

H   The first Canadian astronaut in space

A   A young Canadian who wanted to raise money for cancer research

F   A Métis author

B   A writer who fought for women's rights in Canada

C   One of two scientists who helped discover insulin

D   The first woman Governor General

E   A native actor, poet and public speaker

G   A famous Canadian surgeon

SHORT ANSWER

1. Terry Fox was a young man who wanted to run across Canada to raise money for cancer research.

2. The "Terry Fox Run" is an annual run that takes place each September to raise money for cancer research.

3. Emily Murphy was an advocate of women's rights in Canada. Because of her efforts, women were declared persons under the law.

4. Dr. Norman Bethune was famous because he helped both the Spanish and the Chinese during their civil wars.

5. Dr. Frederick Banting and Dr. Charles Best discovered insulin used to fight diabetes.

Chapter 11: What is Typically Canadian?

TRUE / FALSE

1. F   4. T   7. T

2. T   5. F   8. T

3. T   6. F   9. T

FILL IN THE BLANKS

1. French, English   4. Maple leaf

2. Quebec   5. Hockey

3. Poppy

MATCHING

H "a mari usque ad mare"

E Canada's national police force

A symbol on the Canadian flag

B symbol on the nickel

G nickname for the Canadian dollar

C symbol on the Quebec flag

D symbol of Remembrance Day

F located in Ottawa

SHORT ANSWER

1. A National park is an area of land owned and administered by the federal government. National parks are designed to preserve the wilderness for Canadians to enjoy.

2. Canada is a bilingual country because there are two official languages: French and English. All federal services can be accessed in either French or English.

3. Canada is a multicultural country because its citizens are descendants from many different countries and cultures.

4. Canadians call their dollar coin a loonie because there is a picture of a loon on many of the dollar coins.

5. A goal of multiculturalism is to treat all Canadians as different but equal.

Chapter 12: Becoming a Canadian

MULTIPLE CHOICE

1. A	4. B
2. C	5. D
3. D	6. C

TRUE / FALSE

1. F	4. F	7. T
2. F	5. T	
3. T	6. F	

FILL IN THE BLANKS

1. freedom of religion
2. more
3. responsibilities
4. The Charter of Rights and Freedoms
5. right
6. volunteerism

SHORT ANSWER

1. The freedoms Canadians enjoy are the freedom of religion, the freedom of thought, belief, opinion and expression, and the freedom of peaceful assembly.

2. The rights Canadians enjoy are the right to vote in elections, the right to live and work anywhere in Canada, the right to run in an election, the right to be treated equally, and various legal rights.

3. The responsibilities of Canadians are the responsibility to vote in elections, the responsibility to be loyal to Canada, responsibility to learn and obey the laws of the country, the responsibility to refrain from discrimination against others, the responsibility to participate in the community and to care for Canada's heritage.

4. Freedom of the press means that the news media can print any stories which they know to be true. The government cannot stop them from printing a story.

Suggested Resources for the Classroom

MAPS

To obtain inexpensive maps of Canada and the world for classroom use, call toll free 1-800-465-6277 or write to:

Department of Natural Resources

Canada Map Office

615 Booth Street

Ottawa, Ontario

K1A 0E9

ELECTIONS CANADA PUBLICATIONS

The following publications can be obtained free of charge by calling toll free 1-800-267-8683 or by writing to:

Elections Canada

1595 Telesat Court

Ottawa, Ontario

K1A 0M6

- *Canada at the Polls:* an election simulation kit (includes teacher's guide, supplies for one polling station, documents for counting votes, a set of Elections Canada publications, and a poster).

- *Representation in the Federal Parliament:* an illustrated booklet on the principle of representation in the House of Commons and the process of readjusting federal electoral boundaries.

- *Profile of an Institution:* a brochure describing the history and mandate of the Office of the Chief Electoral Officer of Canada.

- *Voter's Guide:* information on registration and voting in federal elections.

CITIZENSHIP MATERIALS

To order the following publications, call (819) 956-4800 or write to:

> **Canada Communication Group Publishing**
> **Ottawa, Ontario**
> **K1A 0S9**

🍂 *Canadian Symbols Kit*: cards and posters of Canadian symbols.

🍂 *How Canadians Govern Themselves* by Eugene Forsey — information about the federal and provincial systems of government and the constitution.

🍂 *The Charter of Rights and Freedoms*

A Guide for Students,

A Teacher's Manual.

A number of resources including The Canadian Citizen, A Look at Canada, More of a Welcome that a Test: An Instructor's Resource Kit for Adult Immigrant Citizenship Preparation, a poster of The Canadian Charter of Rights and Freedoms, etc. are available from:

> **Citizenship Registration and Promotion**
> **Department of Citizenship and Immigration**
> **15 Eddy Street, 13th floor**
> **Hull, Quebec**
> **K1A 1K5**

Several materials have been produced by the Ontario Ministry of Citizenship and can be obtained by writing to:

> **Citizenship Development Branch**
> **Ministry of Citizenship**
> **77 Bloor Street West, 5th floor**
> **Toronto, Ontario**
> **M7A 2R9**

PHOTOGRAPHS

Pictures of the Prime Minister, the Leader of the Opposition, and Members of Parliament can be obtained from: House of Commons, Ottawa, Ontario, K1A 0A2

A picture of the Governor General can be obtained from Government House, Press Secretary, Sussex Drive, Ottawa, Ontario, K1A 0A1

To obtain pictures of provincial, territorial, and municipal government representatives, contact individual provincial, territorial and municipal government offices.

FILMS

The National Film Board has a wealth of materials that can successfully be incorporated into the ESL classroom. Contact the NFB in your area for films on a wide variety of Canadian topics. The NFB developed a teaching handbook some years ago that has film summaries, lesson plans, exercises etc. for ESL students. Although the handbook is not fully up to date, it has some excellent suggestions for the use of NFB resources. The handbook should be available through your local NFB.

- Smith, Inger (1982). *Teaching English as a Second Language With the Aid of Selected Films.* Montreal: National Film Board of Canada.

CANADIAN MATERIALS FOR ENGLISH AS A SECOND LANGUAGE STUDENTS

Canadian materials for LINC levels 1-3 appear in an annotated bibliography in the *TESL Canada Journal*, Special Issue No. 3, 1993.

References

The Canadian Encyclopedia (1988) Edmonton: Hurtig Publishers Ltd.

Forsey, E. A. (1988). *How Canadians Govern Themselves*. Second Edition. Ottawa: Ministry of Supply and Services.

Government of Canada (1989). *Canada: A Portrait.* Ottawa: Ministry of Supply and Services.

McKie, C. & Thompson, K. (1990). *Canadian Social Trends*. Vols. 1 & 2. Toronto: Thompson Educational Publishing.